WE CAME OF AGE

A Sport Picture History

WE CAME OF AGE

A PICTURE HISTORY
OF THE
AMERICAN FOOTBALL LEAGUE

BY JACK ORR

FOREWORD BY MILTON WOODARD

WITH AN INTRODUCTION
BY MATT SNELL

Acknowledgement

The Editors wish to thank Harold Rosenthal,
head of Public Relations of the American
Football League for his valuable assistance
in the preparation of this book.

Dedicated to sport fans of all ages.

All photos courtesy of United Press International

Published simultaneously in Canada by George J. McLeod Ltd.
73 Bathurst Street, Toronto 2B, Ontario
Printed and bound in the United States of America
Library of Congress Catalog Card Number: 79-86985

1541194

CONTENTS

Foreword. 11

Introduction. 12

1. . . . .THE SEASON. 17

2. . . . .BEFORE THE GAME. 23

3. . . . .THE GAME 26

4. . . . .THE MAN WHO DID IT 37

5. . . . .IN THE BEGINNING 42

6. . . . .A LEAGUE IS BORN 45

7. . . . .TWO GUYS FROM TEXAS. 49

8. . . . .THE BOSTON PATRIOTS. 55

9. . . . .THE KANSAS CITY CHIEFS. 61

10. . . . .THE BUFFALO BILLS. 70

11. . . . .THE OAKLAND RAIDERS. 78

12. . . . .THE DENVER BRONCOS 87

13. . . . . THE HOUSTON OILERS 93

14. . . . . THE SAN DIEGO CHARGERS. 103

15. . . . . THE MIAMI DOLPHINS. 111

16. . . . . THE CINCINNATI BENGALS. 115

17. . . . . THE NEW YORK JETS 123

18. . . . . 1970—ONE BIG LEAGUE. 137

STATISTICS 139

GLOSSARY 151

INDEX 154

PREFACE

Jack Orr's "We Came of Age" is a welcome addition to the sports shelf of every pro football fan, young or old. He offers a true picture of the excitement generated by the league from its inception in 1960 right up through its magnificent triumph in the Super Bowl, in January 1969, when the New York Jets upset the heavily-favored Baltimore Colts.

In the AFL's thrill-filled decade it has not only developed fans for its own league but for all of professional football. It has also developed its own stars who can match performances with the game's greatest, current and past. Such super-stars as Joe Namath and Lance Alworth follow on the heels of trail-blazers as Keith Lincoln, Abner Haynes, Cookie Gilchrist and Don Maynard.

Jack Orr has captured the spirit of the AFL, and all of us in our league congratulate him on this achievement.

MILT WOODARD
President, AFL

New York, 1969

11

INTRODUCTION

BACK in the year 1900, baseball had only one major league, the National League. That was the year the American League was organized. And for a while the newcomers were treated like step-children, but they fought back, and by 1903 they had made their point. The two major leagues squared off in the first real World Series; the "junior league" beat the old-timers, five games to three.

History has a way of repeating it-self. Back in 1960, there was only one pro football major league, the National League. Then the American League began operations, and once more it was a case of the new group being on the outside looking in. But they hung on, and once again a "National League" faced up to the fact that they had competition. And it took a few years longer before the junior league won the football version of the World Series—when the Jets beat the Colts in the Super Bowl game.

Just as the addition of the American League was good for baseball, so it was that pro football as a whole benefited from the new league. More people saw pro ball games; the sport became more popular than ever.

But it's true that the AFL was an inferior league during its first couple of years. It was strictly a wide-open game they played; most of the time defense went out the window, with the passers tossing those heaven-help-us long bombs, the running backs breaking loose—and the defense trying its best to catch up with the offense. It was exciting if you liked high-scoring games, but a little peculiar if you were a student of football strategy.

It wasn't that the coaches weren't capable. They were as good, as knowledgeable as any in the National League. In fact many of them had spent years in the senior circuit as assistant coaches. Nor were the players that much inferior. It was simply a problem of newness. The men had never before played as a team. It's a very difficult job to install a complete system of offense and defense. That is why expansion teams, in both leagues, seldom get out of the cellar for a couple of years. It takes that long before any club "jells."

And the American League wasn't a humpty-dumpty bunch at all. During its formative years the new organization had to pick up its players the best way it could. Most of the time they were forced to accept what was considered second best. Yet they came up with surprisingly good men.

Some of the early American League stars were "retreads," players who had been in the National League for some years without achieving any particular distinction. But when they were given a chance these veterans showed that there was plenty of good football left in them.

Consider George Blanda, who had been an in-and-outer during his National League career. Finally he quit football in disgust. But he joined the American League and promptly began pitching the Houston Oilers to championships. In one season he threw 36 touchdown passes, and that's a lot of TDs no matter which league a man is playing in. And after he became too old to stand there throwing the ball, he became a field goal specialist.

Jackie Kemp is another case in point. He couldn't make it in the National League for the strangest reason on record—his arm was too strong. He threw the ball too hard! Jackie had the ability to heave the leather for a full seventy yards on the fly, and when he rifled those short passes, the ball kept popping out of the receivers' arms like it was a greased pig. Sid Gillman, head coach of the San Diego Chargers, turned things around for Jackie. He simply told the pass catchers that if they couldn't hang on to the ball he'd get new receivers, not a new quarterback. It worked, because the Chargers won plenty of ball games on Kemp's arm.

Len Dawson was another man who came back to the top after a miserable career in the NFL. After being released by the Cleveland Browns, Dawson was given a new lease on life under the benign eye of his former college coach, Hank Stram, who was the head man with the Dallas Texans (later they became the Kansas City Chiefs). Dawson won the American League passing championship no less than four times! Over a five-year period, he threw more touchdown passes than anybody else in pro football, including the great Johnny Unitas over in the other league. Actually, in 1968, the year my teammate Joe Namath was passing the Jets to the championship, the champion passer (by statistics) in the American League was not Namath but Len Dawson.

The American League got some standout players who were cut by National League teams during the training season. Now, I know it's difficult to spot the talent in a young, unheralded rookie, who's trying to catch the coach's eye the best way he can. When there are sixty, seventy or eighty men in camp, many of them tried and tested veterans or bonus players with great college reputations, the free agent hasn't much of a chance. So an unknown pass receiver named Lionel Taylor, from tiny New Mexico Highlands College, failed to stick with the Chicago Bears. But the Denver Broncos took a chance on him, and Taylor, with that great kangaroo leap of his, became an all-league receiver. The Bears had made a mistake —every team in the history of pro football has done the same thing. But fortunately there was an American League operating so that Lionel Taylor could show his skills.

And there were players who were high draft choices in both leagues, but who had decided, for various rea-

sons to go with the young league. Abner Haynes was drafted by the National League, the American League and the Canadian League, but he chose Dallas and became one of the AFL's first super stars. Fred Arbanas was high on the draft lists too, but he went the AFL route, and there isn't a better all-around tight end in pro football today. Other sought-after players who chose the junior football circuit include Ron Mix, Ernie Ladd, Heisman Trophy winner Billy Cannon, Lance Alworth, E. J. Holub, Sherrill Headrick, Mike Garrett and many others, all of whom could win a starting berth with any club in either league.

It has taken several years, a lot of wrangling and much hard work, but now the two leagues are one (as of January 1, 1970). And that is good for pro football. For it should be plain to anyone who watches the game (and, counting the television audiences, that seems to include most of the country) that the American League is at least the equal of the National League in all departments, man for man and team for team. I don't say that just because the Jets bore down and beat the Colts in the Super Bowl, either. All it takes is a close look at the players themselves.

Is there a better all-around quarterback in pro football than Joe Namath? I don't think so, at least not today, when the rubber has gone out of Johnny Unitas' arm.

Running back position? Of course Gale Sayers is a threat to go all the way any time he gets his hands on the football. But you can say the same thing about Mike Garrett. Both are cut from the same pattern.

Interior linemen? I've watched Jerry Kramer of the Green Bay Packers operate, and he sure is plenty good. But I've been racked up by Kansas City's Buck Buchanan and my bones ache every time I think of that guy piling into me.

Pass receivers? They've got a bushel full of good ones sprinkled over both leagues. But the man who holds the pro football record for yards gained receiving passes is my teammate, Don Maynard. In 1968 he broke the record formerly held by Ray Berry (now retired) of the Baltimore Colts, and Don shows no sign of stopping.

Team against team we've proved ourselves in games other than the Super Bowl. The AFL managed to spring quite a few surprises during the 1968 inter-league exhibition season, especially when the lightly-regarded Denver Broncos beat the rugged Detroit Lions, much to the chargin of the supposedly older and more experienced circuit. As for those games we didn't win, well, the other team knew they'd be in a rough game of football.

What excites me most of all is the way we're attracting the younger fans, the pre-teens and the teen-agers. This isn't true only of those American League cities which have no competition in the form of NFL clubs nearby. We're holding our own in those areas when all it takes is a short automobile ride—or the twist of a knob on a television set—to see teams from both leagues in action.

Take New York City for example. Once upon a time, in the dark days when the Jets were still the Titans, pro football fans who were unable to get tickets to see the New York Giants play would drive out deep into Long Island, where the television sets could pick up the Giant home games (blacked out in New York) via stations in Bridgeport, Connecticut. Whole families would check into motels for the day just to watch these games. They could have watched the Titans play without stirring from their homes; but to most New York football fans, the Titans were just a bunch of guys wearing jerseys chasing a pigskin around the field, and who wanted to see them?

Maybe Giant fans still drive out to Long Island these days, but not nearly as many as before. Today, the Jet games are sell-outs too, and when my team is to be seen on the television tube, half the city stays home to watch us. The American League brand of football is tops all the way.

As the years pass, most of the differences between the two leagues will be forgotten. The common draft, which ended the sky-high bidding for college stars and assured all teams of an equal crack at the top talent, will help to even up the relative strength of the clubs. But for me the American League will always be the organization that came up the hard way, a little at a time, fighting its way to the top of the heap. And if anyone doesn't think the AFL is number one, then I wonder where they were in January, 1969, when the New York Jets won the championship of professional football!

Matt Snell

1......■ ■ ■ ■ ■ ■ THE SEASON

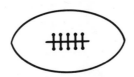

With one-third of the 1968 American Football League season spent, the outlook wasn't brilliant for the New York Jets. They were destined to become champions of the professional football world, but at that particular moment their record was a tremulous one. After victories over Kansas City and Boston in their opening games, the Jets, favored by three touchdowns over the Buffalo Bills, played badly and lost, 37-35. Then after a victory over San Diego at Shea Stadium, 23-20, the Jets inexplicably lost to the weak Denver Broncos, 21-13.

So, late in October, the Jets were in trouble. Their record was a shaky three-victories, two-defeats, and they had lost two of their last three to weak sisters. And their next game was with the tough Oilers in Houston, the team that had beaten them for the division championship the year before. Even the renowned and colorfully glib quarterback, Joe Namath, reflected the gloom. He sat before his locker after the Denver game, his head in his hands, and blamed himself. "Those

interceptions killed us," he told reporters. "Honest, fellas, I don't want to talk. Give me a break. Just tell everybody that I stink."

The Jets' pride seemed to have been dented with the Denver defeat. But the team suddenly pulled itself together in the game against Houston. The Jets took a 13-0 lead, lost it in the fourth period when Houston scored two quick touchdowns—but then came back in the closing minutes as Namath directed an 80-yard touchdown drive. There were no fumbles and no interceptions, a foretaste of how the Jets were going to play the rest of their games.

They won them all, with the exception of the memorable match against the Oakland Raiders, the game that was blacked out for television viewers because the National Broadcasting Company people brought on the children's special, "Heidi."

In that one, the Jets were leading, 32-29, with 1:01 left to play, and the

A grim moment for Joe Namath, after defeat

New Yorkers felt as confident as N.B.C. did. The network cut away, and suddenly the great aerial duel between Namath and Oakland's Daryle Lamonica dissolved, and in its stead, on TV sets everywhere, appeared the delightful Heidi and her gruff grandfather on a Swiss peak. In New York, the viewers went out of their minds. There were so many instant calls to N.B.C. that the switchboard blew a fuse. Frustrated fans then called the New York Police Department, The *Times* and the *Daily News*—and, for some reason, the fire and sanitation departments.

What happened on the field was something New York fans might have chosen not to see. Trailing by three, Lamonica threw a screen pass to the swift Charlie Smith for a 20-yard gain, aided by a 15-yard penalty against the Jets. Then the quarterback again hit Smith with an aerial on the 20—and he sped into the end zone. On the ensuing kickoff, a Jet fumbled the ball and a Raider picked it off and scampered over the goal. New York TV viewers discovered the next day that their Jets had lost, 43-32.

The Jets' disappointment was monumental, but again the team showed its fortitude, defeating the tough San Diego Chargers the following Sunday, 35-15. It was a key victory, virtually clinching the Eastern Division championship. The next three games—against Miami (33-17), Cincinnati (27-14), and Miami again (31-7)—were more or less conditioners for the A.F.L. playoff game against the winner of the Western Division.

That turned out to be their old buddies from Oakland, who had routed Kansas City, 41-6, for the honor of meeting New York at Shea Stadium for the American Football League title and the right to play the National Football League winner in the Super Bowl.

It was a grim, muddy struggle on a day marked by tricky wind gusts—no joke at Shea Stadium where the strong winds are factors in any game. It didn't appear to be a day for outstanding passing performances, even though Lamonica (the league's Most Valuable Player in 1967) and Namath

(MVP in 1968) were to pitch against each other. But despite the 40-mile-an-hour gales, together they tried 96 passes, and the record crowd of 62,627 huddled against the chill and cheered them on.

For a while it appeared that neither passer was going to connect. In the opening period, Namath had three completions of 12 attempts; Lamonica three of 15. But one of Joe's aerials followed a very short Oakland punt into the howling wind—and caught all-league end Don Maynard for a touchdown. Later, Jim Turner kicked a 33-yard field goal, and at the end of the period, the Jets led, 10-0. But Lamonica, a finely honed field general, began moving the Raiders on short passes to his running backs and to his splendid flanker, Fred Biletnikoff. After only a minute of the second period,

Biletnikoff outsmarted the Jets' Johnny Sample and scored a 29-yard touchdown on a Lamonica pass. Then New York got three back on Turner's field goal, but Oakland's veteran George Blanda also kicked one and the Jet lead at the half was 13-10.

In the tricky footing and with the possibility of fumbles, it wasn't much of a lead. But the Jets showed that they considered this their year with pulsating heroics in the third period. The defensive unit held Oakland for three downs inside the Jet six-yard line, forcing the visitors to settle for a field goal that tied the score, 13-13. Moments later Namath took the Jets on an 80-yard drive, highlighted by four dazzling third-down plays—and hitting Pete Lammons, tight end, with a 20-yard scoring pass. That made it, 20-13, Jets.

Matt Snell (41), of the Jets, evades tackle by Oakland's Dave Grayson (45)

Oakland's Daryle Lamonica (3), is jubilant after scoring a touchdown against Kansas City, 1968

Now, in the fourth period, Lamonica connected with Biletnikoff for 57 yards, setting up another Blanda field goal and bringing the Raiders within four points. On the Jets' next series of plays Namath aimed a sideline pass at his favorite target, Don Maynard, but it was intercepted by the fine Oakland cornerback, George Atkinson, who carried the interception to the New York five-yard line. Pete Banaszak took the ball across from there, giving the Raiders a 23-20 lead with less than eight minutes to play. The big, shivering, partisan New York crowd sighed, visions of eight frustrating years dancing in their minds. Oakland had posted ten points on the scoreboard in less than a minute. It appeared to be the end of the line, once again, for the New York A.F.L. team.

Joe Namath, his celebrated white shoes muddied, did not think so, however. Performing with poise and deliberate cockiness, the Jet quarterback hit George Sauer with a short 10-yard aerial for a first down. Then, on the next play, Maynard flew down the sideline with the Oak defender at his heels. Namath faded back, found excellent protection, let go one of his patented passes—and Maynard stuck his hands up 52 yards away—and it was a first down on the Oakland six-yard-line.

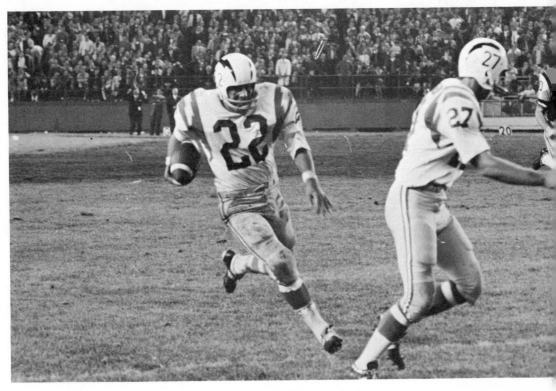

Keith Lincoln (22), of the Chargers, scores a touchdown against the Jets

Len Dawson (16), of Kansas City, in action against Miami

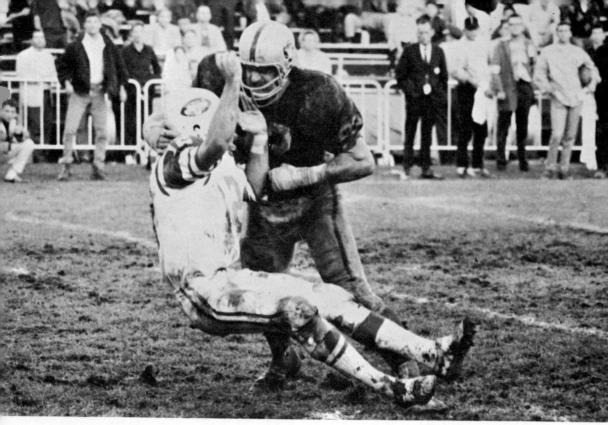

The Jets' Joe Namath is stopped by Ben Davidson (83), of Oakland

On the next play, Joe Namath rolled out as if to take it in himself, but found himself blocked. He looked for Bill Mathis—who was covered. So was George Sauer. Then he threw a bullet to Maynard, who was falling down but caught the ball just as his knees hit the muddy turf. It had taken Namath only 31 seconds to regain the lead, 27-23.

But the Raiders weren't through. They roared back to the Jet 26-yard line and tried a pass on fourth down, but the Jets' defensive end, Verlon Biggs, dragged Lamonica down for a loss. New York used up as much as it could of the time, but with two minutes remaining, the Oakland club still had a chance. The Raiders had the ball, completed two long passes, took advantage of a penalty and were in good position on the Jet 24-yard line.

The play that ensued was the name of the game for the A.F.L. that year. Lamonica faded back. His receivers were covered. He tried to throw a safety-valve toss to his running back, Charlie Smith, but the ball was behind him, making it a lateral and legitimate game for the defenders. Linebacker Ralph Baker of the Jets grabbed the ball and the Jets ground out plays for the final two minutes and a throbbing 27-23 victory.

The Jets, after years of waiting and after being on the edge of the cliff at a point one-third of the way through the season, had prevailed.

They were on their way to the Super Bowl!

2 ■ ■ ■ ■ ■ ■ BEFORE THE GAME

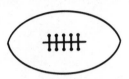

The team the Jets were to play for the pro football championship of the world was the formidable Baltimore team of the established older league. The Colts had been awesome in winning their league's title. They raced through the N.F.L. with only one defeat in sixteen games. They did it without their premier quarterback, the great Johnny Unitas, who injured his arm in an exhibition game and was replaced by a journeyman signals-caller, Earl Morrall. The substitute, working for his fifth club in a thirteen-year career, played so brilliantly that he was voted Most Valuable Player of his league for 1968.

In addition to a breathtakingly splendid offense, the Colts boasted a defense that caused veteran football men to marvel. In the high-scoring atmosphere that is pro football these years, the Colts shut out four opponents, held two others without a touchdown (only field goals) and yielded an average of ten points a game.

In addition, the teams Baltimore played were considered far superior to the teams the Jets had to play in their fourteen games. The National Football League had the strength; the other league worked from weakness.

The one defeat on the Baltimore record had occurred in mid-season against the Cleveland Browns. Scheduled to play their toughest opponent —the Los Angeles Rams—the week after the Brown game, the Colts apparently looked too far ahead and absorbed a 30-20 loss at the hands of the Browns. Subsequently, when the Colts won their division title by impressively rolling over Dallas, 31-20, the Browns won their division title. The teams grappled for the N.F.L. title before 80,000 fans in Cleveland.

Baltimore defeated the only team that had beaten it, 34-0, in a prodigious display of almost flawless football. The Colts' defense was so good that Cleveland's deepest penetration all day was to the Colts' 33-yard line, and that didn't happen until the third period when the game was well in hand for the winners.

Jets' coach Weeb Ewbank

In the week before the Super Bowl game at Miami, the 1968 Colts were being mentioned in the same breath with the great clubs in pro football history. Their coach, Don Shula, was hailed as a genius. Their quarterback, Morrall, was called the "headiest" signals-caller in the game today. Their fearsome front line—Bubba Smith, Billy Ray Smith, Fred Miller and Ordell Braase—represented, it was said, the finest four in demolishing rival quarterbacks. Their linebackers—Mike Curtis, Dennis Gaubatz and Don Shinnick—were said to be fast, ferocious and unbeatable. So were the cornerbacks—Bobby Boyd and Lenny Lyles. The safety men—Jerry Logan and Rick Volk—could not be outmaneuvered.

As for offense, Baltimore had scored 402 points, with Morrall throwing to his superstar ends, Willie Richardson, Jimmy Orr and John Mackay, and handing off to his superstar backs, Tom Matte and Jerry Hill, and if worse came to worst, Lou Michaels was the best field goal kicker in the business.

That was the picture the experts painted for the New York Jets for weeks before the Super Bowl game. "All in all," one wrote, "the Colts are a ball club of coordinated talents, vast depth and boundless spirit, a combination just too much for the Jets to handle." The New York club was dismissed as a "cheese" champion of a "Mickey Mouse" League. One

Joe Namath looks confident as he clowns with Coach Ewbank prior to the 1969 Super Bowl

sports magazine expert predicted a 49-0 rout for the Colts. A broadcaster, known for his tough-minded opinions, said the game was such a mismatch that the result would be "a travesty on the name of pro football." A pool of fifty-five newsmen assigned to cover the match showed that forty-nine of them favored the Colts.

Against this mountain of evidence that they were to be slaughtered, the Jets were surprisingly cool. Particularly nonchalant was the irrepressible Joe Namath, the one they called "Broadway Joe," who lolled at his motel's poolside and told newsmen what the Jets were going to do to the National League champions. He said that Earl Morrall was not as good a quarterback as five or six quarterbacks in the American League. He said that Morrall would be third-string quarterback on the Jets (behind Joe and Babe Parilli). He said that the Colt line was overrated (particularly Bubba Smith, the man-mountain defensive left end). Summing up, Namath told newspapermen: "I guarantee you that the Jets will win."

The experts chortled. The Colts bristled. Bubba Smith said: "He ought to be more like the Green Bay Packers, solemn and humble." Lou Michaels, the field goal kicker, running into Namath in a restaurant one night, threatened to punch him in the nose. (The fight simmered down when Namath picked up Michaels' dinner check.) Coach Don Shula said: "Very interesting, very interesting..." Newsmen and broadcasters dutifully recorded Namath's remarks and the Colt reaction.

That was the atmosphere on January 12, 1969, when Joe Namath led the Jets, three-touchdown underdogs, into the Orange Bowl before 75,377 fans.

3. ■ ■ ■ ■ ■ ■ ■ ■ THE GAME

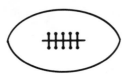

Those were the match-ups as the huge crowd filed into the Orange Bowl that Sunday afternoon. Man for man, the Colts were supposed to be superior in nearly every respect, and those in the crowd who ran down their programs nodded knowingly: the Colt front four will smear Namath; Jet runners will never get moving; the Baltimore linebackers will crush anyone who does get through; the cornerbacks will smother Namath's receivers. As for the Jet defense, it is too small or too young or too old, and when Morrall starts to work on it, it will be the end of the Jets.

In fact, the way the game started out, the Colts seemed ready to substantiate the pre-game opinions. The Jets could not move the ball for a while and then were pushed around. National League fans began thinking this was their day. Morrall passed to John Mackey and Mackey bowled over two Jet tacklers and rumbled for 19 yards. The resourceful Tom Matte swept right end for 10 yards and Jerry Hill went the other way on a

sweep for 7 yards more. Then Morrall passed to Tom Mitchell, his tight end, at the 19-yard line for still another first down.

Up in the stands and higher up in the press box and the television booth and before millions of television sets, the consensus was clear: it's the same old story of National League superiority. Green Bay had defeated Kansas City, 35-10, in the original Super Bowl in 1967, and had walloped Oakland, 33-14, in the second confrontation. Here we go again. The gap between the leagues would remain frighteningly wide for still another year.

But at the 19, the Jet line rose up. Twice Morrall was forced into incompletions. On third down, the lightly regarded cornerbacks, Johnny Sample and Randy Beverly so clung to Colt receivers that Morrall could not find a target and ran for no gain. Lou Michaels, the Colt field goal kicker whose 18 field goals and 48 points after touchdown, made him the third highest scorer in his league, missed on a 27-yard attempt—and that ended

Earl Morrall (15), of the Colts, attempts to pass as Jet Gerry Philbin (81), moves in

the Colts' first drive.

The Jets' troubles weren't over, either. A fumble on their own 12-yard line in the second period, still scoreless, gave Baltimore another fine scoring chance. For the Jets, and their supporters back in New York, it must have seemed that the team was back where it was after a third of the season had gone by: in very shaky straits.

But when Morrall went back on third-and-four and fired a cannon-ball shot pass at end Tom Mitchell, the "Mickey Mouse" defense, as they derisively called it, came through again. The ball struck Mitchell on a shoulder pad, caromed high in the air and Randy Beverly made a diving, off-balance interception, 10 yards away in the corner of the end zone.

Pete Lammons (87), takes a pass from Joe Namath and bites the dust: third period

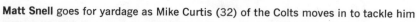

Matt Snell goes for yardage as Mike Curtis (32) of the Colts moves in to tackle him

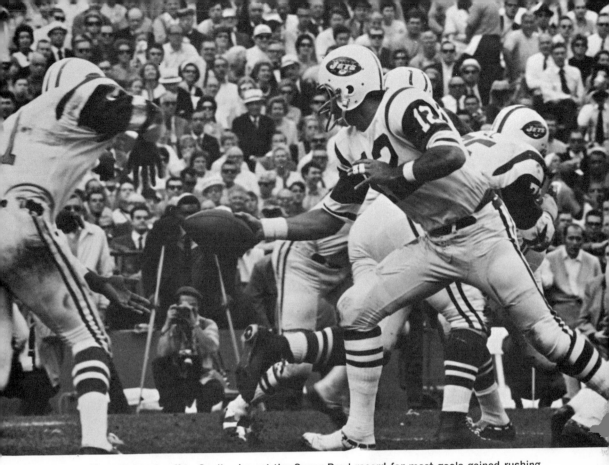

Namath hands off to Snell, who set the Super Bowl record for most goals gained rushing

Despite an injured shoulder, Johnny Unitas engineered the only touchdown drive for the Colts

1969 SUPER BOWL LINEUP

Jets Offense

No.	Player	Position	Ht.	Wt.
80	George Sauer	Split End	6-2	195
75	Winston Hill	Left Tackle	6-4	280
61	Bob Talamini	Left Guard	6-1	255
52	John Schmitt	Center	6-4	245
66	Randy Rasmussen	Right Guard	6-2	255
67	Dave Herman	Right Tackle	6-1	255
87	Pete Lammons	Tight End	6-3	233
12	Joe Namath	Quarterback	6-2	195
32	Emerson Boozer	Running Back	5-11	202
41	Matt Snell	Running Back	6-2	219
13	Don Maynard	Flanker	6-1	179

Colts Defense

No.	Player	Position	Ht.	Wt.
78	Bubba Smith	Left End	6-7	295
74	Billy Ray Smith	Left Tackle	6-4	250
76	Fred Miller	Right Tackle	6-3	250
81	Ordell Braase	Right End	6-4	245
32	Mike Curtis	Left Linebacker	6-2	232
53	Dennis Gaubatz	Middle Linebacker	6-2	232
66	Don Shinnick	Right Linebacker	6-0	228
40	Bobby Boyd	Left Cornerback	5-10	192
43	Lenny Lyles	Right Cornerback	6-2	204
20	Jerry Logan	Strong Safety	6-1	190
21	Rick Volk	Free Safety	6-3	195

Colts Offense

No.	Player	Position	Ht.	Wt.
28	Jimmy Orr	Split End	5-11	185
72	Bob Vogel	Left Tackle	6-5	250
62	Glenn Ressler	Left Guard	6-3	250
50	Bill Curry	Center	6-2	235
71	Dan Sullivan	Right Guard	6-3	250
73	Sam Ball	Right Tackle	6-4	240
88	John Mackey	Tight End	6-2	224
15	Earl Morrall	Quarterback	6-2	206
41	Tom Matte	Running Back	6-0	214
45	Jerry Hill	Running Back	5-11	215
87	Willie Richardson	Flanker	6-2	198

Jets Defense

No.	Player	Position	Ht.	Wt.
81	Gerry Philbin	Left End	6-2	245
72	Paul Rochester	Left Tackle	6-2	250
80	John Elliott	Right Tackle	6-4	249
86	Verlon Biggs	Right End	6-4	268
51	Ralph Baker	Left Linebacker	6-3	235
62	Al Atkinson	Middle Linebacker	6-2	230
60	Larry Grantham	Right Linebacker	6-0	212
24	John Sample	Left Cornerback	6-1	235
42	Randy Beverly	Right Cornerback	5-11	198
22	Jim Hudson	Strong Safety	6-2	210
46	Bill Baird	Free Safety	5-10	180

Jets' Johnny Sample (24), breaks up a pass from Baltimore's Morrall to Willie Richardson (87)—again in the second period

Namath used this break as the springboard for a brilliantly executed 80-yard touchdown drive that put his signature on the game. On this drive Namath began by using his 219-pound fullback, Matt Snell, four times in a row for 26 yards. The long gainer was the draw—in which the quarterback makes as if to fade for a pass but instead hands off to the fullback coming toward the line while onrushing linemen are still trying to find the quarterback—and the Colts fell for it time and again. The Jets' offensive line, particularly Winston Hill, played admirably on this drive. Namath was directing a game that was supposed to be the exclusive property of the National Football League. His team was controlling the ball on a long drive.

Now, with the Colt defense alerted to the Jet running attack, Broadway Joe, as they were calling Namath, went to the air. Baltimore had geared its defense against Don Maynard, the slip of an end, who had caught 10 Namath touchdown passes during the season. So Namath threw to the other wide receiver, George Sauer, for a first down. Then he hit Bill Mathis, in for Snell, on an outlet pass for six more yards, then came back to Sauer in the cracks of the zone (where one defender takes over responsibility from another defender), once for 14 yards and again for 11. The Colts had not expected Namath to throw much to his running backs, figuring that he would have to keep them at home to protect him from Baltimore's pass rush. But now Namath hit Snell for 12 yards, down to the Colt 9-yard line. With utmost calm, Namath went back to the running game and Snell carried twice, barrelling into the end zone

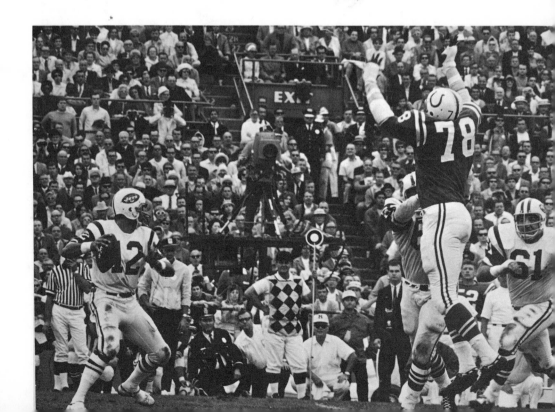

on the second attempt from four yards out. It was a pretty play, Snell starting to the inside, then veering out, with the help of a slashing block by Winston Hill.

Jim Turner's conversion made it 7-0 with ten minutes to go in the first half. Baltimore, the prohibitive favorite, began losing its poise. Morrall, the player of the year, panicked.

He threw in desperation. Every smart-aleck crack ever made about the American Football League as a basketball contest came back to taunt the partisans of the old league. The Jet defense kept him busy. Once, on a razzle-dazzle play, one of the last plays of the half, the Colts had a splendid chance. Morrall handed to Tom Matte on a sweep to the right—a play which had been effective for Baltimore—and Matte, in mid-sweep, stopped and threw a long lateral back across the field to Morrall. Far downfield in the corner near the goal line, Jimmy Orr was jumping up and down and waving his arms frantically, completely overlooked by the Jet defense. But Morrall did not see him and threw over the middle into a crowd of players—and Jim Hudson, the Jet strong safety, leisurely nipped in ahead of Colt Jerry Hill to intercept. Later in the period, when Baltimore was moving again, a Morrall pass intended for Willie Richardson on the Jets' 2-yard line was intercepted by the jazzy and talkative cornerback, Johnny Sample, who had been dumped by the Colts, a team he had played for in earlier years. Sample leaped to his feet with the ball and tapped

Emerson Boozer (32), gets a hand-off from Joe Namath

Richardson on the helmet with it. Then he shoved the ball in the Colt's face. "Hey, man," said Sample, "this what you're looking for?"

So the half ended with the preposterous Jets ahead by a touchdown. On the first play of the second half, they recovered a Matte fumble and Jim Turner kicked a field goal to make it 10-0. When the Jets stopped the Baltimore offense again, Namath engineered another drive to the Colt 30, where Turner kicked another three-pointer.

At this point, with some three minutes left in the third period, Baltimore called on Johnny Unitas, the master quarterback who had spent the season on the bench nursing his injured elbow. He showed some of his old spark, passing the Colts to an 80-yard touchdown drive, culminated by a

Namath stays cool while the Colts' Bubba Smith (78), attempts to block a pass

one-yard plunge into the end zone by Jerry Hill. By this time, though, with the Jets sitting on a 16-0 lead, there was not much concern about Johnny U.'s attack.

But when Lou Michaels converted, making it 16-7, and when the Colts' Tom Mitchell recovered an onside kick at the Jet's 44-yard line—with more than three minutes to go in the game—the situation got tighter. Unitas moved the Colts, on three straight passes, to the New York 19. There the momentum died. Three passes, one intended for Willie Richardson and two for Jimmy Orr, fell incomplete, and the Colts were done for the day and the season. They had been beaten fairly and squarely. There was nothing flukey about it. No mirrors, no sleight-of-hand, no magic—just hard-nosed, convincing football that made believers out of the countless of thousands of skeptics.

In the locker room after the game, the Jets gloated a fourteen-carat gloat, understandably. Dismissed as clowns and basketball players and "Mickey Mouse" blockers and defenders, they had subdued a team that was supposed to be the finest National Football League in a decade.

Said Joe Namath: "Well, I hope nobody expects me to come on with the 'humble bit.' I always have confidence. If you don't have confidence, you shouldn't play this game. A guy who doesn't have confidence just doesn't come from a good family." One of the writers asked if he were sorry for Morrall. "Better him than me. What do you think people would

have said of me if we had lost?"

How about the "ifs" of the game, if the Colts had held on to a couple of interceptions, if Morrall had spotted Orr alone near the goal line, if they had got on the scoreboard first? "Well," said Joe Namath, "I always think this about 'if': if a frog had wings he wouldn't bump his behind." Other Jet heroes chimed in. "Morrall had to play catch-up football," said Matt Snell, "and he didn't look like a catch-up quarterback, did he?" Larry Grantham, a linebacker who had made an unassisted tackle on the Colts' mighty John Mackey, was told that nobody is supposed to bring Mackey down alone. Grantham said: "Guess I'm a better man than he is." Randy Beverly said: "I'm glad we handled The Old Master (Unitas) as well as we did the other fella."

The winners told jokes. Johnny Sample, the Jet cornerback, said: "I think the National Football League will be ready for our league in two years." Former Yankee pitcher Whitey Ford was in the locker room and somebody spotted him: "Hey, Whitey, we knocked out their starting pitcher." And somebody else, in an aside to a reporter, said, "How many shutouts was that going to be for Baltimore"—referring to the N.F.L. boast that the impregnable Colt defense had registered four defeats in which the other team hadn't scored.

In the shocked dressing room of the Colts, praise for the Jets did not come easily. The Baltimore players blamed themselves for the defeat, just barely conceding that Joe Namath

Defensive back Mike D'Amato (47), congratulates coach Weeb Ewbank after Super Bowl upset

had a good arm, that the Jet secondary played superbly and that the offensive line did exceptionally well.
Coach Don Shula did say, "Namath's
quickness took the blitz away from us
so we weren't able to contain him,"
but most of the Colts' comments ran
along the lines of "we didn't play our
game." Superstar Johnny Unitas had a
novel excuse: "It's The Man Upstairs
who really controls this game and if
that's the way He wanted it to be,
that's the way it turned out."

"I guess he meant that The Man
Upstairs likes guys with long hair
and big mouths, who wear Fu Manchu mustaches, mink coats and white
shoes," said one reporter leaving the
Unitas interview.

✻   ✻   ✻   ✻   ✻

In the post-game discussions the
red-faced experts, who had made Baltimore such a decisive favorite, clam-
bered out of the way as gracefully as

Super star of the Super Bowl—Jet Joe Namath

they could, but not too gracefully. The expert who thought that Colts-by-49 had a nice ring to it before the game, decided that his team had been overconfident. One Baltimore writer thought: "The worst part of the Colts' shocking downfall in the Super Bowl that humiliated the entire National Football League was the aftermath in which the Jets proved such ungracious, bad-mouthing winners. The mean-mouthed Jets have upset two athletic institutions at once—the N.F.L.'s cherished prestige and the sports tradition in all fields that it is the worst possible bad manners to crow and jeer loutishly at those you have beaten." (None of the writers who followed this line put into perspective the fact that the Jet comments came as a result of the pre-game abuse they and the American Football League had taken as an inferior group, a league that supposedly didn't belong on the same field with the superior National Football League.)

Other writers used a time-honored ploy of disclaiming their predictions by referring to the game as one in which the Jets "showed up the experts," present writer, of course, not included. Still another excuse was to blast poor old Earl Morrall, the journeyman who had played so nobly in leading the Colts to 15 victories in 16 games. "Everybody who said he was a bum in the first place turned out to be right," that line of dissecting ran.

One red-faced N.F.L. thinker showed considerable class by naming himself as one of those slinking out of Miami quietly after the game. First he publicly apologized for his narrowness as a football seer, then he turned around and stated forcefully that the Jets, except for Namath and few others, "were no better than the Denver Broncos." He heard about that from countless readers who hit the sports editor with bags of letters. "Namath is certainly a singular athlete of superstar stature," one ran, "but it was not Namath who intercepted four Baltimore passes for the Jets or completely outmaneuvered the Baltimore pass defense. It was not Namath who provided the extraordinary pass protection which allowed the same Namath the time to pick his receivers. It was not Namath who so harried the Colt quarterbacks that their passes were rushed, resulting in inaccurate throws and interceptions. And it was not Namath who carried the ball to set a Super Bowl record—that was Matt Snell."

Regardless of the alibis, the fact remained that the two leagues were of equal stature after that January afternoon in 1969. Even the alibis—the Colts would have won if this or that play had worked—underlined the point. The A.F.L. was younger and had the coming stars, while the N.F.L.'s aces (Unitas, Sonny Jurgensen, Bart Starr) were nearing the end of their careers.

4■ ■ ■ ■ ■ THE MAN WHO DID IT

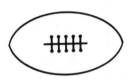

Joe Namath, the architect of the Jets' victory over the Colts, was, at the time, a complex 25-year-old who had in four seasons established himself as a folk hero of the new generation. Not only had he proved himself as a superstar on the field but he had also kindled the imagination and spirit of the young off the field by his coolness, his freshness, his honesty and his brashness. He became a New York personality practically overnight back in 1965, when he was signed by the Jets' show-business-minded co-owner, David A. (Sonny) Werblin, to a three-year contract worth $400,000.

Joe's troubled knee is viewed for the first time at a press conference

Namath receiving some instruction from Coach Ewbank

From that day on, Namath's name was seldom out of the newspapers, even during the off-season.

There were up-front news stories about his knee operation, follow-up stories on his progress, feature stories about how much mail he was getting and *Time* and *Life* devoted spreads to the new glamour boy. When he was released from the hospital, Namath took a plane ride back home and was photographed kissing a stewardess. The picture was page-one material all over the country. Whatever Joe did, in fact, was fodder for the columnists, the television commentators and the cartoonists. Even Bob Hope had a quip: "With that kind of money, Namath'll be playing quarterback in a business suit."

Back in New York, even as a rookie, Namath continued to attract attention. He became part of Manhattan's swinging upper East Side bar and dis-

cothèque scene, patronized in the main by single girls and bachelors. He took a two-bedroom penthouse apartment, complete with Victorian chairs, a Swedish chandelier and 18-karat gold bathroom fixtures. He outfitted it with a nine-inch high white llamaskin rug. He threw extensive parties. Wherever he went in town, he was in danger of having his clothes torn off by over-exuberant fans, most of them young.

And on the field, Namath was living up to most of his notices. From his first year, when he was named American Football League Rookie, 1965, to that overcast Super Bowl Sunday in 1969, when the world of professional football was turned upside down almost singlehandedly by Broadway Joe —he had been a dominating force in the game. By the end of 1968, though he had played about half as many years as his peers, Namath was the second-best All-Time passer in the league's history.

Joseph William Namath was born on May 31, 1943, in a racially mixed section of Beaver Falls, Pennsylvania, a drab steel town twenty-eight miles northwest of Pittsburgh. His father, a Hungarian Catholic who immigrated here at the age of twelve, worked in the steel mills. Joe was the youngest of a family of four boys and a girl, and since there was little to get by on, he shined shoes, caddied on the golf course and did odd jobs. He once told of stealing golf balls "not because I was a thief but because we needed the money." Once, when Joe was 11, his father took him through the steel mill where he worked. The boy, though a veteran of the streets and not easily scared, was terrified. Many years later he was to say: "I knew I could never work in the mill. I knew I had to get out."

Sports was a way to get out. And Joe was good at them all. In an area filled with good athletes, he was the most outstanding in every one. He was pursued by baseball and football scouts, but because his mother wanted him to go to college, Joe went that way. He was turned down by the University of Maryland because of his grades, but the legendary Paul (Bear) Bryant at Alabama heard about him and soon Joe was enrolled there. Though unhappy at first, resented by classmates because he might take the quarterback job away from an Alabaman, Joe soon became a campus favorite. (He turned down an offer of

. . . **and the knee** again keeps him out of an exhibition game against the Oilers in 1968

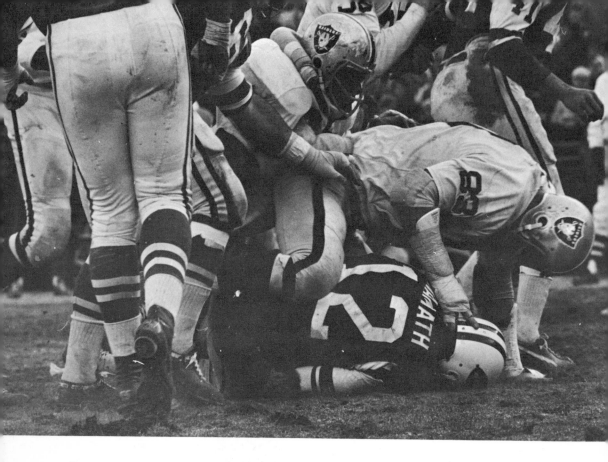

Namath is smothered by five hundred pounds of Kansas City beef

$50,000 to sign as a pitcher with the Baltimore Orioles.) And in his three years, he led the university to three bowl games and Alabama lost only three regular-season games. By now, of course, Namath was the most beloved man in the state, where they take football with utmost seriousness, and when Bear Bryant kicked Joe off the squad for breaking training, he had to go on statewide television to explain why he did it.

Then came Namath's transition to Manhattan, the $400,000 bonanza and the continuing travail that besets his knees. There was betting that he wouldn't get through the first training season, so bad were those knees. He had injured the right one in college and had had cartilage dug out before reporting to the Jets. But it still pained him and there was no telling when it might go again. In one of the early games he came up with an inflamed tendon in the other knee. The word spread around the league early: blitz him any time you like; you'll know where to find him because he can't run.

Four years later they were still saying that, but not with as much con-

viction. For despite the knees and despite the immobility, the fact remained—as the Colts discovered in the Super Bowl game—Joe got rid of the ball faster than anybody in pro football.

Namath's crowd-pleasing magnetism never was more strikingly demonstrated than when Joe and the Jets returned to New York after the 1969 Super Bowl game. More than 10,000 fans, most of them young people, crowded around the steps at City Hall to send up cheers for the returned heroes, particularly Namath. Mayor John V. Lindsay tried to speak, but the crowd chanting for the Jet quarterback drowned him out. The team drove up-town in a motorcade to more hurrahs, with the emphasis on Namath's name. And when the group reached its destination, a restaurant, it found the place already besieged by young people who shouted, cheered and even wept at the sight of Namath. He was awarded a sports car bestowed on the Super Bowl's Most Valuable Player. Broadway Joe, from Beaver Falls, Pennsylvania, by way of Alabama, had captured The Big Town.

Don Maynard, left, and Jim Turner, right, approve a clean-shaven Joe, who got rid of the fuzz after winning the Eastern title

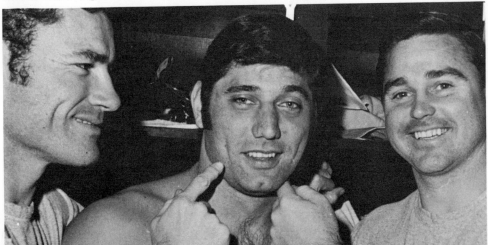

5 ■ ■ ■ ■ ■ IN THE BEGINNING

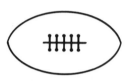

Though on an unorganized basis, professional football can be traced back to the turn of the century. The first pro team was sponsored by the Young Men's Christian Association in Latrobe, Pennsylvania, as early as 1895. Latrobe, not far from Pittsburgh, won the first recorded game by defeating Jeannette, another township nearby. For the next ten years Latrobe played all comers and took whatever purses it could get.

Soon teams were popping up in other sections. In Ohio, which was to be the cradle of hundreds of pro players for two decades, strong teams emerged in Akron, Massillon, Canton, Columbus and Dayton. In New York State, a dozen clubs were formed, among them Buffalo, Syracuse, Watertown, Auburn, Corinth, Oswego and Alexandria Bay. In Pittsburgh, the Duquesne County and Athletic Club fielded one of the strongest teams and was able to draw scores of outstanding collegians to its roster. Many of the college players didn't bother to wait until graduation and either

quit school or played under assumed names.

Among the early players were the great Jim Thorpe, who played for Canton, and his Carlisle Indian teammates, brothers Bemus and Hawey Pierce, who were on the Duquesne team. Others were Doggie Trencherd of Princeton, Walter Okeson of Lehigh, Pudge Heffelfinger of Yale and Arthur Poe, another Princeton star. There were others from Cornell, Dartmouth, Pennsylvania, the University of West Virginia, and one year the entire Lafayette backfield (Best, Barclay, Bray and Walbridge) played for the Greensburg, Pennsylvania team.

In 1902, Syracuse, with its star Phil Draper from Williams College, Glenn (Pop) Warner and his brother Bill and the dazzling Pierce brothers, defeated the Philadelphia Nationals, 6-0, in a novel game at Madison Square Garden, New York City. It was an experiment in indoor football, complete with officials in high silk hats, gloves and spats, but it was not to

Pop Warner

Knute Rockne

Red Grange

catch on. Also that year, baseball's Connie Mack organized a team which he called the Athletics, with his eccentric bad boy, baseball's Rube Waddell, in the backfield. Connie Mack claimed the championship of the world after beating Pittsburgh, which had a fullback, giant pitcher Christy Mathewson, who had been a line plunger at Bucknell.

Charlie Moran, who was later a major league baseball umpire, played for Massillon and, briefly, Billy Heston, the all-time Michigan back, worked for Canton. The Columbus Panhandles, coached by Joe Carr, who later became president of the National Football League (1921-1939), were a strong club and one year six of its starting positions were filled by brothers named "Nesser." None of them ever went to college but rattled around the pro game for many years. Al Nesser, an end, played for the New York Giants in the late 1920s.

By the end of World War I other illustrious names had appeared in pro football lineups: Knute Rockne and Gus Dorais of Notre Dame fame, Tuss McLaughry, Jock Sutherland, Greasy Neale and Charlie Brinkley, the great Harvard drop-kicker (though he lasted only two seasons).

All of these greats laid the groundwork for the organization of the first organized pro football league. Their lot had not been an easy one. For the most part the players were weekday plumbers and truck drivers who only played the game on Sunday. They received $10 to $75 a game (when they got that) and they played before sparse crowds. Their only satisfaction was in playing the grueling game of football. But it was their drive, joined with that of other pioneers with foresight, that laid the basis of professional football as it is known now.

6. ■ ■ ■ ■ ■ A LEAGUE IS BORN

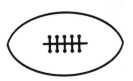

The first professional football league came into existence, in 1919, in a most haphazard way. One hot summer day in the showroom of Ralph Hay's automobile agency in Canton, Ohio, five men agreed to start a league. Hay was general manager of the Canton Bulldogs, and the others were Leo Lyons of the Rochester Jeffersons, Joe Carr of Columbus, Frank Neid of Akron and Carl Storck of the Dayton Triangles.

They called their new baby the American Professional Football League, a name that was changed within two years to the National Football League. Each of the five cities was assessed twenty-five dollars. A code of ethics was drawn up, consisting chiefly of an agreement not to dicker with college athletes until they had completed their courses (an agreement not honored for too long). Jim Thorpe was named honorary president but he soon quit and Carr took over.

By 1922, the National Football League included eighteen teams. The Canton Bulldogs won the champion-

ship, by winning more games than any other team though they did not play all the teams in the league or nearly all. Patronage was spotty, the schedule was unwieldy and franchises skipped blithely around from city to city. The game was a ragtag business in those days, for college football was in center stage and the word "professional" was generally frowned on. Still, the league held together during the lean years—until the appearance of Red Grange of Illinois in 1925. This marked the beginning of respectability for the game.

One of the most successful franchises, despite the drawbacks, was the one issued in 1921 to the Staley Starch Company of Decatur, Illinois. George Halas, a husky young man who had played at Illinois and at Great Lakes Naval Station during the war, was the team's player-coach. In 1921, the Staleys had won the championship with only one defeat, and in 1922, Halas changed the team's name to Chicago Bears. The team was struggling to make money. Halas thought

Otto Graham

Frankie Albert

he had the answer: a super star as a gate attraction.

He found one in Red Grange, the Galloping Ghost, who had become the biggest football star of the era by scoring four touchdowns for Illinois against Michigan in twelve minutes. Before Grange's final college game in 1925, promoter C. C. Pyle (dubbed by a sportswriter "Cash and Carry" Pyle) announced that he had signed Grange to a contract, that he was "Old 77's" personal manager and that he was offering his services to the highest bidder. Halas offered a 50-50 split of the gate and won the bidding. It was the dawn of an era in the pro football business.

In his first game against the Cardinals at Wrigley Field in Chicago, Grange's name drew 36,000 fans, though the game was a scoreless tie. A week later 28,000 came to see him go against Columbus. The Bears then went on tour to show off Grange. They played seven games in eleven days, including one which probably saved the franchise for New York.

Timothy J. Mara was a hustling lad who had grown up on the Lower West Side of New York, had quit school to become a newspaper delivery boy at 13 and later developed a lucrative bookmaking business. He was offered a piece of the New York Giant franchise for $500 and though he had never seen a college or professional football game, he accepted the offer in August of 1925.

It looked like less than a wise investment that fall, as week after week, the Giants went deeper in the red. Crowds were around the 15,000 mark when the going was good—and half of those had free tickets given away by press agents and Mara. But the Grange game took hold and the old Polo Grounds in upper Harlem bulged with 79,000 fans the day he and the Bears came to town to thrash the Giants, 19-7. It was the biggest football crowd New York had ever known.

All in all, Grange's appearance as a pro had put a stamp of approval on the game and the league continued to grow from that episode on. (The fol-

Jim Thorpe

lowing year C. C. Pyle formed his own American Professional Football League with Grange as the star of the new New York Yankees. It was the first of many attempts to unseat the National Football League as the major organization of the sport. But despite Grange and teams in Philadelphia, Chicago, Boston, Los Angeles, Cleveland and Brooklyn, among other places, it was a fizzle. The league folded, and Grange later returned to the Bears and played six more seasons. Three of the clubs of the challenging league were absorbed by the National League: New York Yankees, Buffalo, Cleveland, but they were not to stay long. In all, nineteen pro football teams conceded financial defeat between 1926 and 1927.)

Throughout the Thirties, and despite the depression, the National League continued to stabilize with a minimum of franchise shuffling. In 1933, the league was split into Eastern and Western divisions with the winners of each playing for the title, the Chicago Bears defeating the New York Giants in the first playoff game at New York, 23-21.

And as the National League began to achieve a sort of prosperity, other forces followed C. C. Pyle's lead and attempted to establish rival leagues.

In 1936, another league was formed, again calling itself the American Football League. Some of its teams lasted two years, the life span of the league itself. They were: Boston Shamrocks, played two years, champions in 1936; Brooklyn Tigers, 1936 only; Cleveland Rams, 1936 only; New York Yanks, two years; Los Angeles Bulldogs, 1937 only and undefeated champions; Pittsburgh Americans, two years; Rochester Tigers, two years after originating as the Syracuse Braves and moving to Rochester where they were joined by the Brooklyn Tigers early in 1936; Cincinnati Bengals, 1937 only.

Another attempt was made in 1940, at the beginning of World War II. It was also an American Football League and included Columbus, Milwaukee, Boston, New York, Buffalo and Cincinnati. It, too, quietly folded after its second year, with Boston bowing out after a single season.

But the most serious challenge to the established league came after World War II with the formation of the All America Football Conference. The post-war atmosphere was conducive to a feeling of "the more the merrier." Under the beneficent influence of "52-50" (veterans who couldn't find employment were eligible for $50 a week for a year), hundreds of thousands of young men had the time and the spare cash to attend ball games.

The All America Conference lasted for four years and resulted, generally, in increased football salaries, improved playing facilities and bitter rivalry all around. But actually there was an uneven balance of both NFL and AAC teams in the same cities.

New York, for instance, had four: Giants, Yanks, Bulldogs and Dodgers. Chicago had three: Bears, Cardinals and Rockets (later renamed Hornets). The new Cleveland Browns, the most exciting team of the new conference, replaced the old Cleveland Rams. The Rams moved all the way to Los Angeles, and the other All America Conference teams struggled mightily for the period the league lasted. They ran into difficulties immediately. Miami dropped out after only one season, but Baltimore was added. This lineup held through 1947 and 1948. In 1949 the Brooklyn franchise was merged with New York to form a seven-team league.

It was the end of the road for the Conference. The National League graciously allowed the Cleveland Browns (who had won the All America Conference championship for all four years), the San Francisco 49ers and the Baltimore Colts to become National Leaguers. The New York entry was also eligible for absorption, but the Yanks quit after a disastrous time in Dallas, after the 1951 season, leaving the National League in firm control until the next onslaught came in 1959—by another American Football League.

7. ■ ■ ■ ■ TWO GUYS FROM TEXAS

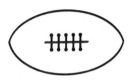

It is generally agreed that the American Football League came into being only because two sons of wealthy Texans were unable to get National League franchises for their very own. Lamar Hunt wanted a club in Dallas and Kenneth S. (Bud) Adams wanted one in Houston. Hunt played the chief role.

Son of the fabled H.L. Hunt—whose income is said to be $200,000 a day—young Hunt was only 26 and just three years out of Southern Methodist University (where he was third-string end) when he decided to have his own football club. At first he tried to buy the Chicago Cardinals—a team running a bad second to the Bears in Chicago—with the view of moving that franchise to Dallas. But Bears owner George Halas, head of the National League's expansion committee, told Hunt that the league would not look favorably upon a shift to Dallas because a team had failed there in 1952.

Thus rebuffed, and used to having his own way, Hunt decided to start a league of his own. He knew that Adams, son of the chairman of the huge Phillips Petroleum Company, also had football visions for Houston. Hunt asked Adams: "If I line up some other franchises for a new league, would you come in?" "You bet," said Adams, and the ball was started rolling by two of the richest scions in Texas history.

So it was that in August, 1959, six representatives of potential franchises in a new professional football league met in Chicago. Besides Hunt and Adams, they were Bob Howsam of Denver, whose family owned the Denver Bears baseball club; Max Winter, E. William Boyer and H. P. Skoglund, three widely respected civic leaders in Minneapolis; Ralph Wilson, Jr., of Detroit representing Buffalo; Barron Hilton, son of the hotel giant, Conrad Hilton, of Los Angeles, and Harry Wismer, the radio and television announcer, heading a New York franchise group. Each group put up a performance bond of $100,000 and the die was cast. (Later,

Lamar Hunt—a man with millions, a dream, and a new league

Minneapolis, Boston, Buffalo, Miami, Louisville, Denver and New Orleans— in other words, practically every city Hunt and his group had considered.

This was the situation when Bert Bell died. Halas repeated that the National League was moving into Houston and Dallas. But Hunt, aroused by now, was undeterred and went ahead with his own plans. When new commissioner Pete Rozelle announced that Dallas and Minneapolis (Minnesota) had been given franchises, the American League sued, charging the National League with monopoly and conspiracy in the areas of expansion, television and the signing of players. The suit was thrown out . eventually, with the National League vindicated and the American League ordered to pay court costs.

The new league went ahead on several fronts:

First, it managed to complete a draft of 1959 college football players. Of the eight that were drawn, however, only three went with the infant league. The other five stayed put, in the greener — they thought — N.F.L. pastures. As a matter of fact, rosters were made up mainly of rookie talent plus Canadian League exiles, along with a handful of veteran players with National League experience.

Playing talent, however, was largely an unknown quantity. As a result of training-camp tryouts, more than 800 players were signed. This number was cut down to the legal limit, 33 players per team, a total of 264.

Second, it named as commissioner Joe Foss, one-time governor of South

the Boston Patriots, with Billy Sullivan representing a ten-man syndicate were added.)

Next, Hunt relayed a message, hinting of his plans but not revealing names or sites, to Bert Bell, then National League commissioner. He found that Bell was not unfriendly to the new project. On the other hand, the Bears' George Halas, overseeing expansion for the National League, seemed ready to throw up whatever roadblocks he could. He said his league's expansion plans included

Three new league coaches, left to right: Frank Filchock, Denver; Sammy Baugh, New York; and Buster Ramsey, Buffalo

Dakota, Congressional Medal of Honor winner, and a man highly respected for his honesty and candor.

Third, it replaced the on-again-off-again Minneapolis franchise with one for Oakland, California, owned by a syndicate headed by Y. C. (Chet) Soda.

And it was also decided that the new league would have a "two-point option," a rule that allowed a team scoring a touchdown a choice of kicking a placement for one point or running or passing for two points.

Early in 1960 the new league was set. The first game was played in Boston, September 9, 1960. Denver, which had not been able to win a single exhibition game, upset the Patriots, 13-10, and the game set the tone for the kind of game the American League was going to show in its first season. Defense was ragged, tackling haphazard and play generally listless. This was the case throughout the league that first year and almost everywhere the offense was ahead of the defense, leading to scores such as 42-41, 35-33 and 28-26. Already they were beginning to call it a "kookie" league.

The Houston Oilers ran away with

the "Eastern" division title and faced the Los Angeles Chargers in the championship game. Ben Agajanian kicked two field goals to give the Chargers a 6-0 lead in the first period and then added another to make it 9-0 midway in the second. But Houston took the lead when Dave Smith scored on George Blanda's 17-yard pass and Blanda kicked the conversion and a field goal for a 10-9 halftime lead. Bill Groman scored for Houston on a 7-yard Blanda pass in the third period, with Blanda converting. But Los Angeles made it 17-16 on Paul Lowe's 2-yard smash, with Agajanian converting. And then Billy Cannon scored on an 88-yard pass from Blanda, who added the extra point for a final score of 24-16.

After that first season there was some rearranging to do. Barron Hilton moved his club from Los Angeles to San Diego. Every club lost money and the only thing that kept the weaker franchises from fading out of sight was a five-year television contract with the American Broadcasting Company. Under the arrangement set up by the league, all TV moneys were thrown into one pool and split evenly among the clubs. Since the first year called for a payment of $1,785,000, it meant a dividend of about $200,000 for the hard-pressed clubs.

Attendance averaged 16,558 for the opening year and rose to 17,864 the following year. But it was not enough to hold off additional heavy losses. In 1962, however, attendance shot up to 21,481 a game and four clubs broke into the black. It looked as if the league wasn't doomed after all. The season was climaxed by an unprecedented sudden-death game between Dallas and Houston that went two extra periods before Dallas won, 20-17. (In the second year playoff, Houston had defeated San Diego, 10-3, on Billy Cannon's touchdown and George Blanda's field goal.)

In the 1962 game, Dallas (champion of the "East") faced Houston ("West") and it was slam-bang football, played with a recklessness that apparently had become the American League hallmark. In the first half, with swift Abner Haynes as flanker, Jack Spikes and Curt McClinton as fullbacks and Len Dawson as quarterback, Dallas took a 17-0 lead. They proceded to lose that edge and the teams were tied 17-all at the end of the game. There was a scoreless extra period and then, in the second extra period, at "sudden death," Tom Brooker kicked his second field goal of the game from the 25-yard line, after 12 minutes of the period. Haynes was outstanding in scoring two touchdowns.

After that third American League season, there was further shuffling. Lamar Hunt, who found that Dallas apparently would not support two pro teams, moved his club to Kansas City, where attendance picked up sharply.

And in January, 1964, in the move that undoubtedly was the turning point in American League fortunes, Commissioner Joe Foss signed a new television contract with the National Broadcasting Company. It called for

$36,000,000 for TV rights for five years, 1965 through 1969. David A. (Sonny) Werblin, who had taken over as co-owner of the New York Jets and who had a show business background with the Music Corporation of America, helped pave the way for the lucrative contract.

Meanwhile, the fight for players continued and bonuses and salaries skyrocketed. Werblin himself pulled a coup when he signed the brilliant Joe Namath of Alabama to a $400,000 three-year contract and probably got that much publicity out of it. But owners in both leagues were beginning to be distressed at the spiraling wage scale. Some kind of peace would have to be established before wages shot out of sight completely.

American League owners, early in 1966, became disenchanted with Joe

Foss, despite the life-saving TV contract he had negotiated. The anti-Foss group charged (a) that he had lost the city of Atlanta to the other league, (b) that he wasn't on top of the situation as far as drafting talent went and (c) that he had bumbled in handling a strike of the league's black players before the All-Star game in New Orleans in 1965. This group wanted a more aggressive commissioner, who would be willing to wink at secret drafts and who would wage all-out war against the other league.

Foss, an honest man, got the message and resigned in April, 1966. He was replaced by Al Davis, head coach and general manager of the Oakland Raiders, a more belligerent type. ("We'll fight for players," Davis said, "and we'll do anything at all we think is necessary to get the job done.")

Members of the AFL expansion committee discussing probable franchise sites with then commissioner Joe Foss

About this time the National League committed an act of provocation. The New York Giants announced that they had signed Pete Gogolak, the field-goal kicker of the Buffalo Bills, who had played out his option. (Under pro football rules, a player usually signs for one season and gives the club an option on his services for the next one. But if he so desires, a player may refuse to sign and play for another year, at a ten per cent cut in pay, after which he becomes a free agent. This is what Gogolak had done.) Still, American Leaguers considered it a "raid" and Davis began plans for counter-raids on National League players whether they had played out their options or not.

At this point in the warfare, peace movements were under way on both sides. Owners were wringing their hands at orbiting bonuses. The time was critically near for merger talks.

The two leagues united in 1966, putting a halt to the raiding. Under an umbrella organization—still to be called the National Football League —each league would still retain its identity and would continue to function as before. A common draft was set up stating that only one team would get negotiating rights to college players, thus putting an end to one league outbidding the other. In other words, the merged league would handle all business transactions, but the two leagues would continue to play against each other, as before.

At this time it was therefore decided that Pete Rozelle, National League commissioner, would become commissioner of the unified league. Al Davis resigned and Milt Woodard, former assistant commissioner and secretary-treasurer, became American League president.

There was some delay in consummating the merger when the owners were threatened by anti-trust action, but the astute Rozelle went to Washington and sold Congress on the merits of one pro football league. As a result, the new expanded league won limited immunity from anti-trust laws when sports-minded Congressmen tacked an amendment onto a bill to suspend investment credit tax. The merger was home free.

For the fan, of course, the most important by-product was the Super Bowl, a meeting of the champions of both leagues, which started after the 1966 season. Regular season interleague play was scheduled to begin in 1970, inasmuch as the American League's television contract, running through 1969, prevented it from starting before that.

Two new franchises, one in each league, were added. New Orleans and Atlanta began play in the National League in 1967 and Cincinnati joined the American League the following year. By 1970, the league was to present twenty-eight teams in twenty-seven cities (only New York having two franchises) and both leagues were to be on equal footing, no matter how the schedule was to be worked out. The American League had come of age.

Gino Cappelletti (20), Boston, an ace receiver, was one of the early stars

8. ■ ■ ■ ■ THE BOSTON PATRIOTS

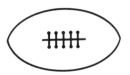

In their first nine seasons in the American Football League, the Boston Patriots usually huffed and puffed behind the leaders of their division. But in 1963, their first season as tenants of Fenway Park, home of the Boston Red Sox, the Patriots showed great tenacity in scrambling to the Eastern title and a spot in the championship game.

That year was the Patriots' fourth in Boston and despite an opening season in the cellar, they had climbed to second place in both following years. Boston fans had rewarded the club with an attendance average of close to 25,000, even though games were played at the Boston University field with a limited capacity. (In one game against Dallas, President Billy Sul-

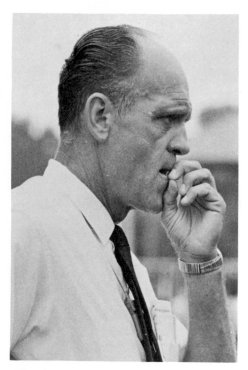

Mike Holovak built the team

livan had, with great sobs, turned away 10,000.) But now the Patriots were to play in Fenway Park with a seating capacity of 38,000 and things were looking up.

On the field, the team was stronger, too. Mike Holovak, who had become coach midway in the second season, had worked to improve the defensive backfield. The offense was directed by the veteran quarterback Babe Parilli, acquired from the Oakland Raiders in a key deal two years earlier. His receivers included Gino Cappelletti, a split end and field goal kicker, and Art Graham, the Patriots' No. 1 draft choice who had been captain of the Boston College team. De-

Jim Nance (35), goes up and through the Miami line

Art Graham (84), goes down over McCloughan of Oakland in a 1965 night game

Larry Garron (40), is stopped by the Buffalo Bills in 1964.

Babe Parilli (15), gets set to pass against the Jets a year before he was traded to the Jets

fensively, three men won All-League ranking: Tommy Addison, middle linebacker; Larry Eisenhauer, end, and Houston Antwine, a tackle picked up from Houston.

The Patriots didn't exactly overwhelm their division—they wound up with a 7-6-1 record—but it was good enough to tie the Buffalo Bills for first place. And along the way, the Boston club had some very good afternoons. Parilli, though often hobbled by a bad arm, won key games against New York, Oakland and Houston. But Buffalo finished strong enough to tie the Patriots and force a division playoff.

That game, played in sub-freezing temperature at War Memorial Stadium in Buffalo, showed Boston at its best. With Ron Burton, the tiny halfback, in action for the first time in four months, with Parilli throwing brilliantly, and with Cappelletti kick-ing four field goals and two conversions, Boston won in a breeze, 26-8. And the defense, rising to the occasion, held the Bill's rushing offense, led by the fabled Cookie Gilchrist, to only seven yards for the day.

In the championship game against San Diego, however, the Patriots left their vaunted defense in the dressing room, and the Chargers, led by the unstoppable Keith Lincoln, rolled up a spectacular average of 9.9 yards on the ground and a 51-10 victory. Boston went home licking its wounds.

The following year the Patriots were in contention again, despite a floundering start. By December, the Eastern title was between them and Buffalo and they met in the showdown game. Boston was a slight favorite, mainly because of Parilli, chosen All-League quarterback, and Cappelletti, chosen Player of the Year for his league-leading 155 points. The Patriot defensive specialists were honored as well: Eisenhauer, Addison and new man middle line backer Nick Buoniconti.

But on a freezing and snowy afternoon at Fenway Park, Jackie Kemp of the Bills had one of the best days of his career. He wheeled his team to a 24-14 victory, accounting for an astonishing 286 yards in the air, as the Boston defenders skidded on the frozen field.

That was not the last hurrah for the Patriots in the first nine years of their existence. Two years later, in 1966, they made a strong challenge for the division title, with their fine fullback, Jim Nance of Syracuse, shining brightly. With two games left on the schedule, the Patriots had to play Houston and New York, and win both, for the title. They took Houston in a breeze, but then ran into the Jets' Joe Namath on a hot day, lost, 38-28, and thus bowed to Buffalo by half a game.

From then on though, Boston fell into doldrums. The team won only three games, finishing in the cellar, in 1967, and only four games a year later.

At the conclusion of the 1968 season, Coach Mike Holovak was fired, and replaced by Clive Rush, an assistant coach of the Super Bowl Champions, the New York Jets. Since then, Rush has made some important player trades to strengthen the team.

Harry Crump (31), gains against San Diego in a game in 1964

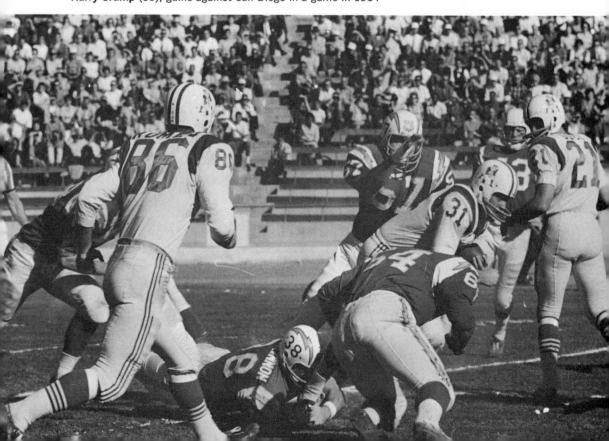

9. ■ ■ ■ ■ ■ KANSAS CITY CHIEFS

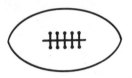

When Lamar Hunt established the Dallas Texans as the American Football League entry in his home town, he found the going very rough indeed. The Dallas Cowboys had the town very well in hand. At the end of three years he still was drawing badly and the word was that he was losing close to a million dollars a year. The story goes that when his father, H.L. Hunt, one of the richest men in America, heard about it, he said: "At that rate, he'll be broke in a hundred and fifty years."

Young Hunt wasn't waiting to go broke, though. And despite two second places and a league championship at Dallas, he moved the franchise, lock, stock and players' bench, to Kansas City, where he won one championship (1966) and three second places in six years.

Both in Dallas and Kansas City, coach Hank Stram has had his share of heroes. Abner Haynes, for instance, in the very first year of the league's existence, was such a versatile and resourceful back that he was named both Player of the Year and Rookie of the Year, a dual honor never duplicated. Other heroes over the years included Mel Branch, Sherrill Headrick, Dave Webster, Jerry Mays, E.J. Holub, Dave Grayson, Bobby Bell, Buck Buchanan and John Robinson, on defense, and such luminaries as Chris Burford, Fred Arbanas, Mike Garrett, Bob Holmes and Frank Pitts. And, of course, Len Dawson still stands on top as one of the all-time great passers in the history of the league.

With that talent over the years, many people have asked, why didn't the Dallas–Kansas City entry win more than two championships? The fact seemed to be that the club was more than erratic in its first two seasons. Then, when it won the championship in 1962, in the historic six-period, "sudden death" game against Houston, the club moved to Kansas City. Since many of the team's key players were Texans and had Texas ties, morale dipped. Also, in training camp that first year in Kansas

Coach Hank Stram talks to Pete Beathard (10)

City, a promising rookie named Stone Johnson, out of Grambling College, suffered a fatal injury—a tragedy that weighed heavily on many of the young players, particularly Abner Haynes, who had been Johnson's buddy.

So that first year in K.C., the Chiefs lost seven and tied two of their fourteen games, and the following year they wound up with seven victories—seven defeats. In 1965 they still could win no more than seven games as San Diego continued to dominate the Western division, capturing its third straight title. Coach Stram came in for a good deal of criticism since, as was pointed out, he had superior personnel. But Hunt stuck with his coach despite everything.

Johnny Robinson (42), hits Houston's Alvin Reed (89)

Stram's indoor lessons were intensive

Len Dawson (16), of Kansas City in action against Miami, 1967

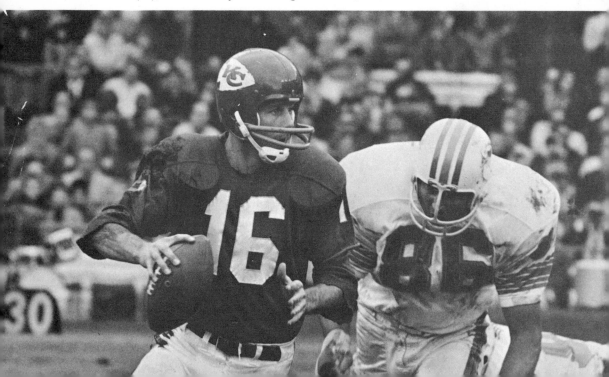

In 1966, with the addition of Mike Garrett, the swift back, and the development of flanker Otis Taylor, the club came to life, winning its last seven games and posting an 11-2-1 record to run away with the division title. Dawson was the league's best passer, and Garrett was second only to Jim Nance of Boston in rushing.

In the championship game against Buffalo, played in the East before 42,080 fans, a record crowd for a title game, the Chiefs were never better. Though the Bills were supposed to have the best defense in the league, Kansas City kept them off balance with a series of different formations, and in the fourth period, Garrett scored twice in a minute-and-a-half to sew up the victory. The score was 31 to 7.

The victory, worth $5,308.39 to each Chief, also made Kansas City eligible for the first Super Bowl game

K. C.'s Bobby Bell (78), takes New York's Don Maynard out of bounds in a 1968 game

Mike Garret squirms past Buffalo defense

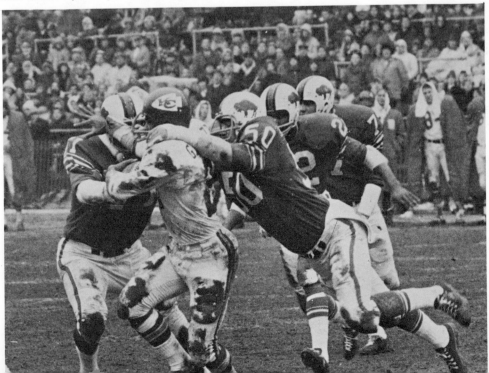

Mike Garret (21), of the Chiefs, evades the Chargers

Kansas City's Otis Taylor (89), receiving Dawson pass against Denver, 1

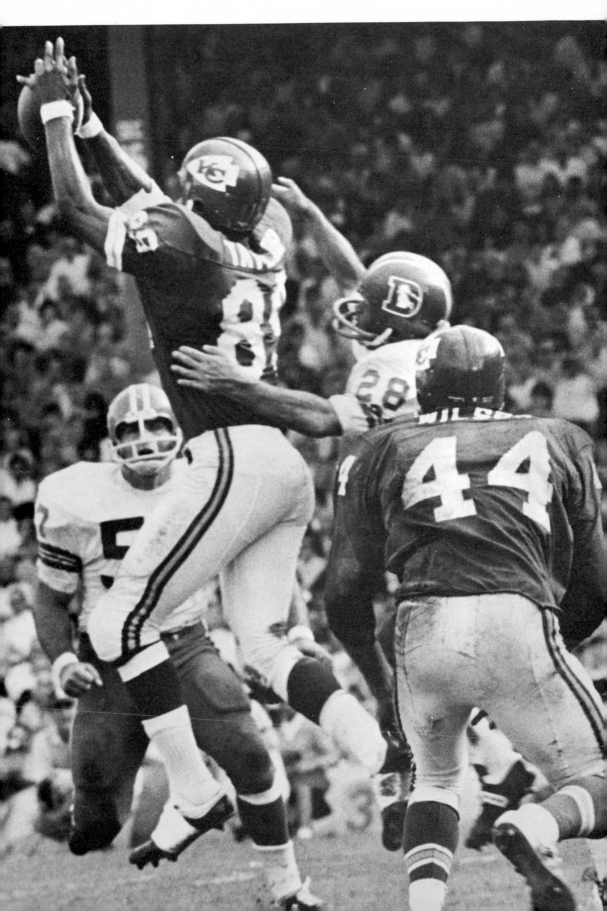

Despite the action, the pass was incomplete and no interference charged

A great catch by G. Richardson (30), in a scoring play against Oak

against the Green Bay Packers. The tilt was set for the Los Angeles Memorial Coliseum and was televised by both the major networks. The pregame hoopla built up an unprecedented tenseness, even shriller than subsequent Super Bowls because this was the first confrontation between the leagues. It was more than pride, too. Winning players each were to get $15,000—losing players, $7,500.

For a half, the Chiefs made a ball game out of it. Dawson, behind 7-0, hit Garrett, Otis Taylor and Curt McClinton for long gains on a 66-yard drive and tied the score. Then Green Bay stormed back for another touchdown, but a Kansas City field goal made it 14-10 at the half. In the third period, the Packers began a systematic blitz of Dawson, dumping him for losses three times. An interception by Willie Wood set up another Green Bay score, then a pass to Max McGee gave them still another. The final score was 35-10, but it was the beginning of interleague rivalry, a foreshadow of games to come.

It was to take the American League two more years before its representative would defeat the club from the older, established league.

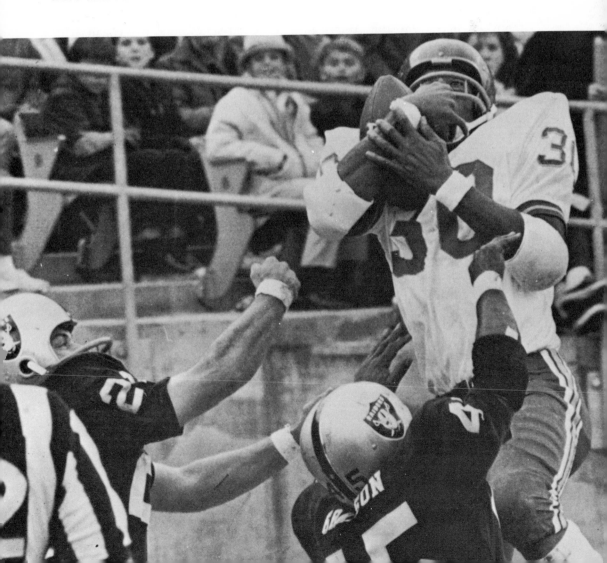

10... ■ ■ ■ THE BUFFALO BILLS

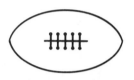

The city of Buffalo has a pro football tradition that goes back fifty years. As early as 1920, the Buffalo All Americans played in the American Professional Football League, which became the National League, and Buffalo played off and on in that league until 1929. Later, in 1940, a Buffalo team was part of the ill-fated American Football League that lasted only two years. Buffalo was an important cog in the workings of the four-year All-American Football Conference which collapsed in 1949. But though the older league absorbed three teams when the A.A.C. folded, Buffalo's bid for a franchise was rejected, mainly, it was said, because of the city's fierce winters. The bid was turned down, even though 25,000 fans had signed a petition, forwarded to the league office, with each signer guaranteeing to buy a season ticket.

Football had been dormant in Buffalo for a decade when Ralph C. Wilson, a wealthy Detroit insurance executive, arrived on the scene, at the behest of Lamar Hunt, in 1959. The enthusiasm was still there, however, and Wilson hired two top football men. The coach was Buster Ramsey, an eight-year defensive coach with the Detroit Lions. The general manager was Dick Gallagher, a knowledgeable professional who had been Paul Brown's chief scout at Cleveland and who had high marks in the matters of evaluating and recruiting players.

The pickings, however, were very thin for Gallagher and the Bills. They had started six weeks behind the other clubs in the new league and as a result the collegians they were able to nab and the veterans they were able to retread were hardly of first caliber. Defensively that first year, the team wasn't bad (thanks to Ramsey's acknowledged talent) and end LaVerne Torczon, linebacker Archie Matsos and defensive back Richie McCabe made the All-League team. But on the offense, the team had no capable quarterback and only one outstanding runner in Elbert Dubenion, who scored eight touchdowns,

Cookie Gilchrist (34), as rugged and rambunctious on the field as he was off

Pete Gogolak (3), kicks one of his better field goals in a 1964 game

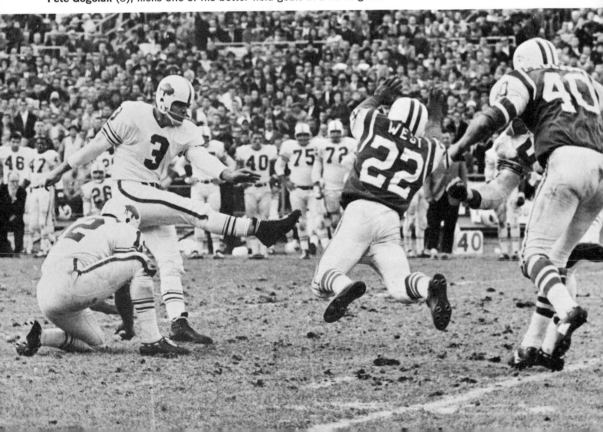

six of them on runs of more than forty yards.

The Bills won five games in their opening season and six in their second, dropping to last place in the Eastern Division in the confusion. That was the end of Buster Ramsey as coach and Wilson hired Lou Saban, a one-time Cleveland linebacker and a deposed coach of the Boston Patriots. Saban shook up the lineup considerably, raided the ranks of the Patriots for assistant coaches and began a rebuilding job. Results were not apparent at once, for the Bills lost their first five games. But Wilson did not give up on his young players or his new coach and this impressed the athletes.

About this time, the Bills acquired a whirlwind: a big, blockbusting fullback, Carlton (Cookie) Gilchrist,

New coach in Buffalo's second year: Lou Saban, who began a rebuilding job

Ralph C. Wilson arrived from Detroit and gave a shot in the arm to the Buffalo sports scene

Joel Collier was dismissed as head coach of the Buffalo Bills, after their worst defeat (48-6), by Oakland early in the 1968 season

six-two, 243 pounds, and a character calculated to get his name in the papers. He had never played college football, only in high school in Brackenridge, Pennsylvania, and in his one tryout with the Cleveland Browns he had failed to make the club. He went to Canada and became a big man, not only on the field but in his free-time escapades.

Cookie played for five clubs in Canada, getting put off each one because of an altercation with his coach. On one occasion when he and the coach were squaring off for a fist fight, Cookie quipped: "You take the first punch, you're the coach." Everybody laughed and the fight never came off.

But despite the shenanigans, the word on Cookie Gilchrist was that he was a rugged, destructive fullback, a devastating linebacker, who could kick field goals from 45 yards out. Cookie admitted that he was good. "There's nothing in football I can't do," he often said.

By now, the Bills had acquired a good quarterback in Jack Kemp, who somehow had been allowed to get away from the San Diego Chargers. After five games, the club got going, with Kemp passing and Gilchrist rolling up yardage, and it won seven and tied one of its last nine games. The following year, 1963, the team improved further with the picking up of a second quarterback, Daryle Lamonica from Notre Dame. With Kemp and the new man, the Bills had gone from a position of no quarterback to a position of having two of the best. Again the club got off badly (Gilchrist was injured early in the year) and lost four of its first seven games. Then the Bills came to life, won five of their last seven to gain a tie for first in the Eastern division with the Boston Patriots. Buffalo lost the playoff, 26-8, but the fans were far from discouraged. They had turned out on an average of 30,000 a game and were anxiously anticipating 1964.

It was even better than that, for the Bills ripped off three straight Eastern division titles. In the first year, with Cookie Gilchrist running up impressive rushing statistics and Jack Kemp throwing well (with Lamonica as his alternate quarterback), the club won twelve games of its fourteen. In the playoff against the tough Western division winner, San Diego, Buffalo rose to new heights. The Bill defense was superb and gave the Charger quarterback, Tobin Rote, a rugged afternoon. Kemp passed expertly, Gilchrist accounted for 122 yards on the ground and the new man, soccer-type field goal kicker

The Jets move in, as Jack Kemp (15), gets off a quick pass for Buffalo

Bobby Burnett (21), a Rookie-of-the-Year, goes around his own left end against Oakland in a 1966 match

Pete Gogolack, kicked two field goals. The final score was 20-7, and the Bills were champions of the league.

Outstanding in this era was the Buffalo defense. The front four—Ron McDole, Jim Dunaway, Tom Sestak and Tom Day—gave up only four touchdowns on the ground for the entire season.

In 1955, when the Bills won their second title in a row, they also dispatched their leading ground gainer, Cookie Gilchrist, to the Denver Broncos. Gilchrist thought he was being overlooked by quarterback Kemp one afternoon and not only sulked and at one point refused to take the field, but when he did perform, he blocked so laxly that the opposition swarmed all over Kemp. Saban fired Cookie two days later, reinstated him at the request of the rest of the team, but then got rid of him for good.

Without Gilchrist, the Bills still were something to see. Kemp had a remarkable year, even though his two best receivers, Elbert Dubenion and Glenn Bass, were knocked out with injuries early in the season. Buffalo won the Eastern title by five full games. Then, facing the dangerous Chargers of San Diego again in the championship game, the Bills faced their sternest test. San Diego that year had the league's leading passer in John Hadl, the leading rusher in Paul Lowe and the best pass receiver in Lance Alworth. None of them fazed Kemp, who had a personal score to settle with the Chargers because they had released him on waivers three years earlier. Kemp ran a masterful game. He completed eight of nineteen passes for 155 yards, Gogolak's field goals came when needed and the Bills won, 23-0—the first time

San Diego had been shut out in four years.

Now two-time champions of the entire American League, the Bills faced the unprecedented goal of a third straight title. And they faced it without their coach, Lou Saban, twice named best in the league. Saban had quit to coach at the University of Maryland and the job went to defensive specialist Joel Collier.

Collier had his problems. Gogolak had jumped to the other league and the Bills needed a field goal·kicker. The running backs were getting on in age. There was need for an explosive rusher. The problems were solved like magic; a place kicker named Booth Lusteg, with no college experience, developed into a master. Several rookies, including end Bobby Crockett, flanker Ken McLean and rusher Bobby Burnett (Rookie of the Year), came of age suddenly. The team, after a faltering start, began winning steadily, and the Bills won their third straight division title in a close race. It was not decided until the final weekend of the season when Boston, half a game behind, lost to the New York Jets and the Bills won their game with Denver.

They came to the end of the line, though, in the league playoff with Kansas City, with the Super Bowl bid at stake, losing, 31-7, and though Collier continued to present a formidable defense in 1967, the club skidded to a third-place finish. In 1968, en route to a 1-12-1 season, the Bills replaced Collier with Harvey Johnson, a poor soul who had been director of player personnel. The players were inexperienced and helpless, but there was still hope in Buffalo. They had had their three years of glory and fans were predicting that those years would come again. And they certainly would, coupling the appointment of John Rauch as the new coach with the addition of O.J. Simpson, one of the greatest of football stars.

Elbert Dubenion (44), one of the first and best of the Bills

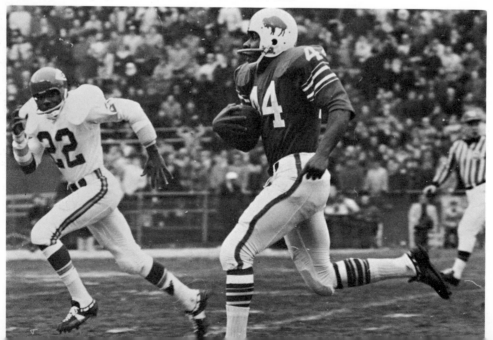

The future looks brighter after the drafting of O. J. Simpson, the greatest college player in years, shown here with the Heisman Memorial Trophy, 1968

11.▪▪ THE OAKLAND RAIDERS

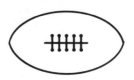

Few football teams in pro history had as disastrous a send-off as the Oakland Raiders in 1960 when the American Football League played its first season. For one thing, Oakland did not get its franchise until two months after the other clubs in the league and as a result had a raggedy draft list of collegians nobody else wanted. For another, the club was owned by eight Oakland civic leaders, all of them pulling in different directions. To top it off, the club had no home field, and was forced to play in San Francisco's Kezar Stadium, home of the Raiders' rivals across the Bay, the 49ers.

Still, despite the handicaps of few big league players and bickering owners, coach Eddie Erdelatz, longtime head coach at the Naval Academy, produced surprising results that first year. With Tom Flores, of the College of the Pacific, and Vito (Babe) Parilli, a five-year National League veteran, alternating at quarterback, and with some capable running backs in Billy Lott, Tony Teresa and Jack Larscheid, Erdelatz led the team to a quite respectable six victories in fourteen games and managed to escape the cellar in its division.

But Bay Area fans weren't exactly nuzzling the Raiders to their bosoms. First at Kezar and later in the year at Candlestick Park, attendance was terrible. Less than 50,000 fans showed up for the entire 1960 season.

When the second season started with two straight thumpings, at the hands of Houston (55-0) and San Diego (44-0), the Raiders fired Erdelatz and replaced him with an assistant coach, Marty Feldman. It didn't help and the club won only two of fourteen games and finished dead last. Attendance at Candlestick continued to drag. A decision was made to play home games in Oakland, rather than across the bay in San Francisco. A new municipal stadium was scheduled to be built, but it would not be ready for a few years. So beginning in 1962, the team played in an inadequate park called Frank Youell Field.

The Raiders lost their first thirteen games that year, insuring them a last-place finish again. And added to the six straight defeats at the end of the

Men on the move—and fast—as Upshaw (63) leads the way against K.C.

Davis came in as coach and general manager

previous year, the club now had lost nineteen straight. Injuries hobbled the few good players. Morale was at an all-time low. Feldman, the coach who had replaced Erdelatz, was in turn replaced by another assistant, Red Conkweight. And on the last day of the season, the Raiders snapped their losing streak on two touchdowns by Clem Daniels against the Boston Patriots.

For the following season, the Oakland owners made a catch that was to send Raider stock up for years to come. They hired Al Davis, a young assistant coach in San Diego, to come in as head coach and general manager. An aggressive man with superconfidence in his own abilities, Davis began rebuilding the club, both on the field and in the front office, and the results were apparent almost immediately. Davis convinced Art

1968 and whoopee! Rookie Charlie Smith (25) is overwhelmed by teammates and coach John Rauch after scoring on a 43-yard pass

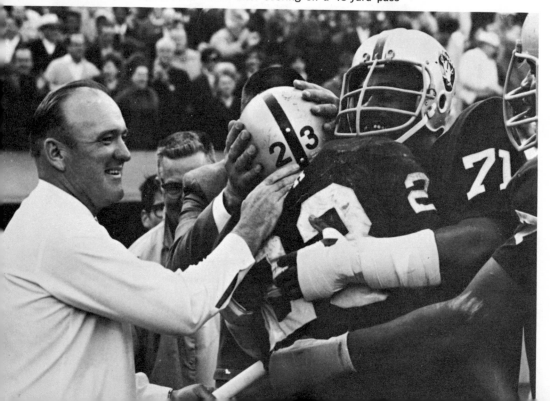

ewitt **Dixon** (35) takes a block from Upshaw (63) in Oakland against the Patriots in 1968

Powell, a flanker, who had played out his option with New York, that things were looking up in Oakland. Davis also leaned on fullback Clem Daniels, who became Player of the Year, and used Flores and Cotton Davidson as alternate quarterbacks. The team began to look like something.

The Raiders got off impressively with an opening game victory over the tough Houston Oilers, 24-13, in Texas, and then came home to defeat the Buffalo Bills, 35-17. Al Davis, in two games, had won twice as many games as Oakland had won the previous year. Then came a bad slump of four games and fans thought things had been too good to last. But Al Davis put the club back on the track and rattled off impressive victories each week for the rest of the season.

The key game arrived late in the year with San Diego, who was leading the division. The situation stood this way: if San Diego won, it would clinch the division title. If Oakland won, it would draw within a game of the leaders and then each club had two remaining games.

Oakland played brilliantly, coming from behind, 27-10, in the fourth period with a 31-point attack that demolished the league leaders, 41-27. It has been said that this scoring explosion—seen by a record Oakland crowd of 20,249—saved professional football for the city. Five times the defensive team took the ball away from the rugged Chargers and each time the offensive team, led by Cotton Davidson, put points on the scoreboard. In less than twelve minutes, the Raiders scored four touchdowns and a field goal.

But San Diego still had its one-game lead and even though Oakland won its remaining two games (for ten straight victories), San Diego won its remaining pair as well and edged the Raiders for the division title. Still, it was a remarkable performance for Al Davis and Oakland. Their ten victories represented more triumphs than the team had won in three previous seasons.

In subsequent years, Davis continued to build for the future with some success. Among his prize catches in the draft were tackles Harry Schuh of Memphis State, Bob Svihus of the University of Southern California, Rich Zecker of Utah State and fullback Gus Otto of Missouri. He also snagged the dazzling Fred Biletnikoff, from Florida State.

But injuries and bad breaks kept the Raiders from enjoying a title until 1967. In 1966, Davis was hired as league commissioner, and took over from Joe Foss, who had resigned. John Rauch, offensive coach, took over for Davis as head coach. Davis returned to Oakland a few months later as one of the principal owners and Rauch continued at the helm with Scotty Stirling as general manager.

The team opened its season in the brand-new 33-million-dollar Oakland-Alameda County Stadium in 1966 and drew well, but again it was a frustrating year, with Kansas City romping to a three-game division title over the Raiders, who finished second.

Oakland ace Daryle Lamonica (3) gets off a short one against the Jets in the 1968 AFL Title Game

Biletnikoff—the dazzling Fred—prepares to complete a pass against San Diego

Hewitt Dixon (35) was one of the sparks that got the 1968 season rolling

The Raiders' Roger Hagberg sprints through a Cincinnati attempt. Biletnikoff (25) moves out of the w

In preparation for the 1967 season, Davis again revamped his team, sending Tom Flores and Art Powell to Buffalo for Daryle Lamonica, the quarterback, and split end Glen Bass. It was a masterful trade, for the Raiders relentlessly swept through the league's Western division, taking thirteen games in fourteen starts. Lamonica was voted the Most Valuable Player, and seven other Raiders were chosen to the All-Star team: fullback Hewritt Dixon, center Jim Otto, guard Gene Upshaw, defensive end Ben Davidson, defensive tackle Tom Keating, cornerback Kent McCloughan and placekicker George Blanda.

In meeting Eastern division titlists, Houston, in the American League playoff, for the right to play in the second Super Bowl, the Raiders never played better. They pounded out a 17-0 halftime lead, then extended that to a 40-7 crusher. But in the Super Bowl, against the mighty Green Bay Packers, Oakland bowed meekly, 33-14.

The Raiders were back in the thick of things in 1968, when they engaged in a ding-dong battle for the Western division title with the tough Kansas City Chiefs. Both clubs won twelve and lost two to finish the season in a tie and necessitate a playoff for the division crown before battling the New York Jets, the Eastern division winner, for the league title.

The Raiders were at the top of their form for Kansas City. The resolute defense held the Chiefs for seven plays on the Oakland three-yard line, and the offense, sparked by Lamonica,

Eddie Erdelatz—Oakland's first coach

ripped off 22 first downs and a 41-6 victory. The flashy Fred Biletnikoff caught three touchdown passes and Warren Wells snagged two, while Blanda had two field goals and five conversions to the delight of the huge crowd of 53,605.

Against the Jets, however, Oakland found Joe Namath and company too tough to handle and New York ground out a 27-23 victory, en route to its Super Bowl assignment against the Baltimore Colts.

But there was no doubt that Oakland had become a big-time power in professional football—and it had made the grade after one of the most dismal starts in history. Now, under coach John Madden, Oakland fans look forward to increasingly better football.

12. ■ ■ THE DENVER BRONCOS

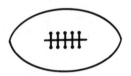

In their first nine seasons in the American Football League, the Denver Broncos boasted a number of fine football players: Lionel Taylor at end, Abner Haynes and Cookie Gilchrist at running back, Gene Mingo (who once led the league in scoring), Wendall Hayes and Billy Joe, Floyd Little, three-time All-American at Syracuse, and Eric Crabtree and Al Denson. The only trouble was that the good players weren't in the club at the same time—and the Broncos have finished in the cellar six times and have never had a winning season.

But their fans have never expected too much from the Broncos. From the beginning the operation was on the penny-pinching side, mainly because there was no money around. The franchise was first awarded to Bob Howsam, of the Denver Bears baseball team, a highly competent baseball executive, his father, Lee, and his brother, Earl. Unlike many of the other owners in the new football league, the Howsams weren't of the super-rich class. In order to ex-

pand the seating capacity of Bears Stadium from 17,500 to 25,000, the Howsams had to pull in their belts.

To staff the new club, the Howsams went to Canada. Dean Griffing, a veteran football front office man in the Canadian Football League, was hired as general manager. Frank Filchock, an old National League man who had spent seven years coaching for Griffing in Canada (Saskatchewan Rough Riders), was named coach. And Frank Tripucka, who had played for Frank Leahy at Notre Dame in the late forties, also was recruited from Canada, where he had played and coached.

The first training camp, at the Colorado School of Mines, in Fort Golden, Colorado, was pretty much a penny-pinching disaster. The players were quartered in an abandoned barracks-type dormitory with no partitions, no closets and beds close together. Clothes were hung on an overhead pipe and everybody lived out of a suitcase. The training table was a grim experience of hash nearly

ny Denver fan will remember Gene Mingo, shown here in '62, going over the goal line

1967. The shuffle turns up Lou Saban, a new coach with a ten-year contract

every night. Scores of rookies came for tryouts and were cut in a few days.

But to everybody's astonishment, the rag-tag Broncos opened their initial season with two victories in a row over the Boston Patriots and the Buffalo Bills. Tripucka still had something left in his throwing arm and completed ten of fifteen passes in the opener and fourteen of twenty-six the following week. Mingo, Taylor and Al Carmichael, from the University of Southern California, were his favorite targets. The team lacked depth, however, and after winning its first home game, it lost all the rest except two and wound up with four victories, nine defeats and a tie.

The Broncos' Billy Joe is going down—but not out—in an early (1964) contest with K.C.

1964. Speedie arrives on the Denver scene

placed, and though the club was virtually the same, it had its finest year in history. Club spirit ran high and the fans recognized it. In the first game that year, 25,000 fans turned out to see the Broncos play San Diego, a team they had never beaten.

Denver turned back the Chargers, 31-21, followed up by defeating Buffalo, and then, after a loss to Boston, went on a three-game winning streak. Then in a game seen by 34,496 fans at Bears Stadium—the largest crowd ever to see a sports event in Denver—the Broncos manhandled the Houston Oilers, two-time league champions, 20-10. That made Denver's record six victories and one defeat, but again its

The Howsams were in trouble, having drawn poorly and lost much money. The club, therefore, was sold to a syndicate of prominent Denver businessmen and civic leaders, headed by Calvin Kunz, president of a large agricultural marketing business, and Gerald Phipps, a local builder. The team did not improve, however, and won only three games of its fourteen. But because Oakland was even worse (two-twelve), Denver climbed out of the cellar.

To shake things up, the new owners fired Griffing, the general manager, and Filchock, the coach, and replaced them with Jack Faulkner, who took over both jobs. Faulkner was more highly organized than the men he re-

1966. And now—Malavasi comes in as coach

Frank Tripucka climbs through the New York Titans line in 1962. Tripucka, a Notre Dame alumnus, shows the Leahy touch

lack of depth cost heavily. The team went into a tailspin, lost its last five games, and finished the season with a seven-seven record. But Faulkner was honored as Coach of the Year and attendance had doubled over the previous year.

The romance was shortlived. The following year, 1964, the team plunged again to the cellar with only two victories and attendance lagged. The fans who had been singing Faulkner's praises the year before, now began yelling for his scalp. They got it. Faulkner was fired early in 1964, and replaced by Mac Speedie, an assistant coach with an alert football mind, who had been an all-time pro end with the Cleveland Browns. But Speedie knew no magic and the team again was held to two victories.

Rumors were afoot that the club would be moved, perhaps to Atlanta, and the rumors spurred interest in the club among Denver residents. Many people who had not been aware of the team now became its biggest boosters and the franchise was served. The acquisition of Abner Haynes from Kansas City and Cookie Gilchrist from Buffalo also helped stimulate interest, for now the Broncos had one of the most powerful one-two punches in the league. Crowds grew again. The average reached 31,398 and talk of shifting the franchise died down.

In 1966, the Broncos lost their opener to Houston, 45-7, and failed to make a single first down, something that had never happened in league history. Speedie was promptly fired and replaced by Ray Malavasi, offensive line coach, for the season which resulted in four victories—ten defeats.

By 1967, the Broncos had brought in Lou Saban, who earlier had been with the Boston Patriots and the Buffalo Bills, but who had become coach of the University of Maryland. He was given a ten-year contract as coach and general manager and a free hand to make deals to strengthen the club. Saban brought three of his assistant coaches—Whitey Dovell, Dick MacPherson and Sam Rutigliano—with him from Maryland and added two others in Stan Jones and Hunter Enis.

There were no immediate miracles. Denver won three games in 1967 and five in 1968, moving out of the cellar because of the league's new franchise in Cincinnati in the latter season. But there were glimmers of hope in the performances of Marlin Briscoe, Fran Lynch, Jim LeClair, Garrett Ford and Floyd Little.

Broncos' owner Gerald Phipps said he was optimistic about the future. "We give credit to the coach, his staff, the crisp organization, and, of course, the common draft and our trades that have worked out well. Also, we have to credit the team's spirit and that of the Denver fans. This kind of support never will hurt you."

13. ■ ■ THE HOUSTON OILERS

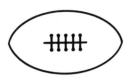

When the Houston Oilers were first being organized for the opening year of the American Football League, Bud Adams, their wealthy and somewhat eccentric owner, sat down with John Breen, his veteran head scout and director of player personnel, to discuss the needs of a team in the new league. They agreed that the basic weakness of most clubs was going to be pass defense and that the club with the superior passing attack was likely to be a winner. It was sound thinking, for it became apparent almost immediately that such was the case when basketball scores began to be run up—45-44, 52-49 and so on.

The Oilers hired veteran George Blanda as quarterback and as the men to mould the younger passers into big leaguers they hired Jacky Lee of Cincinnati and Charlie Milstead of Texas A. & M. Blanda, who had played for the Chicago Bears of the other league for ten years, had in fact retired from football when Adams and Breen decided to hire him. How well he did

is reflected in the American League standings for the first three years. Houston won three Eastern Division titles (thirty-one victories, ten defeats, one tie), won the first two championship games and lost the third to Dallas in a grueling double-overtime game, 20-17. Houston was so successful in its first three years, in fact, that there were those who feared the club was too strong and would dominate the league as the old Cleveland Browns had dominated the All America Conference.

The argument seemed sound, for Blanda had some splendid receivers to take advantage of the other clubs' spotty pass defenses. There was Charlie Hennigan, a wispy 170-pound sprinter who could catch everything in sight; Bill Groman, a little All-America halfback from Heidelberg, who developed into such a fine receiver that he made All League end his first year, and Johnny Carson, from Georgia and the Washington Redskins, with blazing speed and high maneuverability. Working under end

The Oilers' first coach, Lou Rymkus

Hugh Taylor came hard on the heels of Baugh

coach Mac Speedie, they developed into the class of the league's pass catchers.

But perhaps the most significant catch of the pre-inaugural American League period was Bud Adams's successful grab of Billy Cannon. Cannon, who had played college ball at Louisiana State, was a muscular six-footer with speed to burn. He won the Heisman Trophy, signifying the best college player as a senior, and was named to every All America team in both his junior and senior years. He was a prime target for every pro club. Pete Rozelle, now the commissioner of all the pros, was then general manager of the Los Angeles Rams and he signed Cannon to an undated contract before L.S.U. went to the Sugar Bowl in the halfback's senior year. When the season ended, Adams also signed

Cannon to a personal services contract, and Cannon returned his bonus to the Rams and asked to be released from that contract. The Rams said no and took Cannon to court, but the judge ruled that the Ram contract was not valid and that Cannon was free to join the Oilers.

The court victory for the new league was a milestone and it heartened any owners who might be having second thoughts about the success of the league. It showed that the American League could elbow its way in against the entrenched National League and still have a fair shot at winning a point. In fact it set a legal precedent which leaned heavily in the A.F.L.'s favor in subsequent conflict-of-contract disputes.

In the beginning the Oiler coach

Wally Lemm returned to Houston in 1965, has held on ever since

Sammy Baugh, the coach who followed Wally Lemm, who followed Lou Rymkus—telling the press he preferred ranching (1964)

was Lou Rymkus, who had played at Notre Dame under Frank Leahy and who had played and coached in the National League at Washington, Green Bay and Los Angeles. He was a tough, knuckle-down type and a strict disciplinarian.

While waiting for Houston's famed domed stadium to be completed, the one because Blanda missed a field goal from the 28-yard line in the closing seconds when the team trailed Oakland, 14-13, and then ran off five more victories. Heroes emerged, such as Dave Smith, from Ripon College, who became the fullback and the club's leading rusher; Billy Cannon was outstanding; Jacky Lee did a fine

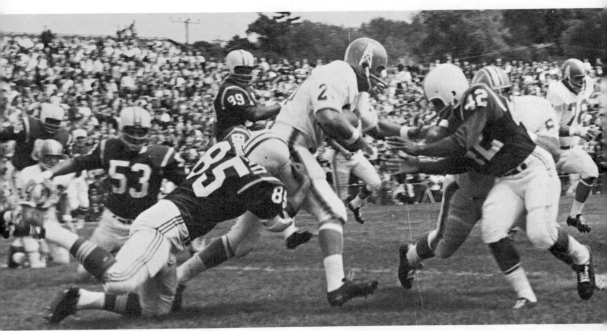

Cannon grabs yards before being brought down by Nick Buoniconti of the Patriots in a 1964 contest

Oilers were forced to play at a high school field, Jeppesen Stadium, which even with improvements could seat few more than 35,000. (The 70,000-seat Rice Stadium was not available to professionals.)

But on the field the Oilers were dazzling. They started off by winning five of their first six games, blew the job at quarterback when Blanda was injured, and Rich Michael was All League offensive tackle.

In the first championship game the Oilers pitted their ten-four record against the Los Angeles Chargers' identical mark. (The following year the Chargers moved to San Diego.) It was nip-and-tuck, with Houston

Bud Adams, Houston Oiler chief, believed that a club with a superior passing attack would be a winner

One of Houston's major inaugural AFL acquisitions: Billy Cannon (20)

Oiler back Zeke Moore (22) is determined to return an Oakland kickoff. 1967

leading 7-6, then 10-9, then 17-16. At this point, Blanda noted that the Charger defense had moved in tight and he sent Cannon out behind it— and the swift halfback gathered in a pass that covered eighty-eight yards for the touchdown that put the game out of the Chargers' reach.

In its second year, Houston opened with only one significant personnel change. It signed Williard Dewveall, a two-year end who had played out his option with the Chicago Bears, and with him aboard demolished Oakland in the opener, 55-0. But then the team went into a puzzling slump, losing three games in a row and being tied in a fourth. The champions were at the bottom of the league standings.

Here, Bud Adams fired the coach, Rymkus, and brought in Wally Lemm, who had been an Oilers' defensive coach during the first year but who had retired to tend to his lucrative sporting goods business. Lemm, a gentler soul than the hard-nosed Rymkus, brought the Oilers back dramatically. It was one of the finest comebacks pro football ever saw.

In their first game, against the hated Texas rivals, Dallas, the Oilers came from behind, 7-0, to win a decisive 38-7 victory. Then Houston went on to win its remaining nine games without a loss for the division title. And in a repeat of the championship game against the Chargers, now based in San Diego, Houston won a bruising battle, 10-3. The Oilers' defensive line harrassed Jackie Kemp, the fine San Diego quarterback, all afternoon, and Blanda, besides kick-

In 1966, George Blanda was still a formidable opponent against New York

George Webster (90), a former Rookie of the Year, hits Jet Bill Mathis hard in a 1968 encounter

ing a 46-yard field goal, also threw an exciting pass, grabbed by Cannon with a superhuman leap, that resulted in the game's only touchdown. The Oilers were champions again, Blanda was named Player of the Year and Billy Cannon All League halfback. End Charlie Hennigan and tackle Al Jamison also made All League on offense, and on the defensive honored team end Don Floyd and linebacker Tony Banfield were named.

Despite his success and his popularity in Houston, Wally Lemm, who had no contract, left Texas the following year to become head coach of the St. Louis Cardinals. Without hesitation, Adams hired Pop Ivy, the coach who had been fired by the Cardinals, to direct the Oilers. It marked the first straight swap of head coaches in history.

Hampered by injuries to Cannon, Dave Smith and Blanda, the team had its difficulties the following year, but somehow it managed to post its best record yet—eleven victories and three defeats—to win the division championship once more. They bowed to Dallas in the historic double-overtime, sudden-death struggle by a field goal.

By 1964, the Oilers were on the skids. True, they had lost the year before when injuries to Cannon and Charlie Tolar crippled the team's running game, but had finished only a game behind Boston and Buffalo, which had tied for the division title. But in 1964 with a new coach, Sammy Baugh, replacing Pop Ivy, the once-mighty Oilers hit bottom with four victories in fourteen games. Only the development of Sid Blanks, a rookie halfback from Texas A. & I., and the promise shown by Don Trull, from Baylor, highlighted the Houston year.

Sammy Baugh quit after the season ended to be replaced by Hugh (Bones) Taylor, who had been an assistant coach under Baugh, and when Taylor took the job he rehired Baugh as his assistant. Soon after this, Lou Rymkus, the original Oiler coach, came back as an assistant, and Walt Schlinkman, who had gone to St. Louis under Wally Lemm, also returned. It was, to say the least, a bit confusing.

The team did not improve under Taylor and again finished last in 1965. Out went Taylor and in came Wally Lemm, returning to the job he had held five years earlier. The club acquired Ernie Ladd, 6' 9" and 315 pounds, from San Diego, and brought in Pat Holmes, 6' 5" and 270 pounds, from the Canadian League. With a roster dotted with many rookies, the Oilers were building for the long haul, but 1966 saw them stumbling again. They battled with the new club, Miami, for the cellar and at year's end both clubs tied for it with identical three victories-eleven defeats records.

But in 1967, the club did improve so enormously that the team went all the way from last place to first. The old hands were traded away without mercy: Blanda, Hennigan, Rich Michael, Fred Glick, Charlie Tolar, all of whom had been All League at one time or other, went to other clubs.

In their places, Pete Beathard, quarterback, was acquired in a trade with Kansas City, and Miller Farr, cornerback, from San Diego. They, plus a horde of brilliant rookies, soon had the whole league talking, as Houston raced to its first division title since 1962. Linebacker George Webster, from Michigan State, was Rookie of the Year. Hoyle Granger (a second-year man) and rookie Woodie Campbell were the rushing terrors. Others were Willie Parker, fresh out of Arkansas A.M.&N., who had to replace the titan Ernie Ladd at offensive tackle when Ladd went in a trade; safety man Kenny Houston, and tight end Alvin Reed. In all, the 1967 squad had fifteen rookies and the situation boded well for the future of the Oilers.

In the championship game that year, however, Houston ran into a hot Oakland Raiders club, directed by Daryle Lamonica, and went down to a 40-7 crushing defeat. But the miracle of going from last place to first wasn't tarnished.

Houston got off badly in 1968, losing four of its first six games, while the New York Jets, inspired by Willie Joe Namath, got off to a big lead with six victories of their first eight. The Oilers ran into some injury woes and were never able to catch up, though most of their fine rookies of the previous season continued to play well. Two new men, Mac Haik and Jim Bierne, became starters at wide end, further evidence that Houston was a solid club and destined to be heard from in the future.

14

THE SAN DIEGO CHARGERS

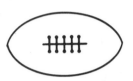

For the first six years of the American League's existence, the San Diego Chargers (originally, for one year, the Los Angeles Chargers) so dominated the Western division that they won five titles. The fact that after this they failed to win for three straight years rubs no luster off that sparkling beginning.

The man who corralled the five titles for owner Barron Hilton, son of hotel man Conrad Hilton, was Sid Gillman, a coach of such singleness of purpose in going after victory that he made most other men in his profession appear to be milquetoasts. Gillman surrounded himself with topnotch assistants, as he had in his earlier jobs

The aftermath: Coach Gillman toasts his players in the locker room after the 51-10 victory

Charger Paul Lowe (23) scores against the Bills in 1965

Coach Sid Gillman, according to most observers, the most single-minded pilot in the AFL

with University of Miami (Ohio), Cincinnati University and the Los Angeles Rams, and together they moulded a superlative team. Two of his assistant coaches, Jack Faulkener and Al Davis, became general managers of other teams. His head of scouting, Don Klosterman, later went to the Kansas City Chiefs and built that team up to championship caliber, and still later did the same thing for the Houston Oilers. At first, Frank Leahy, the Notre Dame former coach, was general manager, but he left shortly after the club was organized and Gillman went his own way in going after championships. In addition to outstanding scouting work by Davis and Klosterman, two of the best talent appraisers in the business, Gillman built a network of 122 college coaches who kept the Chargers informed of promising young players.

Keith Lincoln (22) goes for a 1st down against the Patriots in the 1963 AFL Championship game. Lincoln was named game's most valuable player

As a result, when league play got under way in 1960, the Chargers not only romped away with the division title in the West, but they also placed five men on the All League team, quarterback Jack Kemp, a veteran who had been a reject on three National League teams but who found himself under Gillman; Paul Lowe, an impressive running back who had played at Oregon State; Ron Mix, an All America offensive tackle at the University of Southern California; defensive tackle Volney Peters and cornerback Dick Harris.

The Chargers lost the championship game to Houston, 24-16, that first season and because attendance had been dismal in Los Angeles's vast Memorial Coliseum, Barron Hilton moved the club to San Diego, where he was promised cooperation by the press and by civic groups, something he had not enjoyed in Los Angeles. (Hilton had gone first class that first year, carrying a big payroll and allowing Gillman one of the few "taxi squads" in the league—a group of players who are carried on full salary and who practice all week with the team but are ineligible until injuries make room for them on the active list.) The city fathers agreed to doubledeck the local field, Balboa Stadium, increasing the seating capacity from 20,000 to 34,500 and eventually a 50,000-seat arena, San Diego Stadium, was erected.

For his first season in the South, Gillman had a tremendously powerful team that won twelve games of fourteen, and demolished the rest of the league regularly. Second place in the division went to Dallas, six games behind. Besides Kemp, Lowe, Charlie Powers (a bruising fullback), and new man Keith Lincoln from Washington State, the Chargers had two fine receivers in Dave Kacourek and Don Horton. They also listed All League defensive backs Harris and Charlie McNeil and linebacker Chuck Allen. The same year the Chargers

unveiled Earl Faison, 6'5", 262 pounds, from Indiana University and Ernie Ladd, 6'9", 320, from Grambling, who along with Ron Nerv and Bill Hudson made up the first of San Diego's "fearsome foursomes."

Although San Diego again lost the championship game to Houston in a bruising 10-3 battle, prospects for the following year looked brighter than ever when the club starred a swift graceful back Gillman (turned into flanker), Lance Alworth (who was to be All League for seven consecutive years) and quarterback John Hadl (who was to stay as one of the league's premier signal-callers from then on). But despite the club's strength, injuries hobbled the Chargers and through a clerical error (somebody put the wrong man's name on

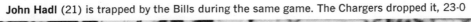

John Hadl (21) is trapped by the Bills during the same game. The Chargers dropped it, 23-0

San Diego's Jack Kemp (15) fumbles the ball in a rare moment against the Raiders, 1962. In 1960, he had made the All-League Team

the draft list) they lost quarterback Kemp to Buffalo—and the club finished with a four-ten record and third place in the division.

But in the following two seasons, San Diego bounced back with a vengeance, winning two division titles and one league championship, a 51-10 trouncing of Eastern winner Boston in 1963, but losing the 1964 playoff to Buffalo. (That result, a 20-7 score, was almost written on the wall beforehand. Alworth, the league's best flanker, suffered a knee injury in the last game of the season, and Keith Lincoln cracked a rib in the first period of the playoff. The Charger offense never did move after that.)

Then in 1965, despite some troublesome holdouts by star players and the first full season for Hadl at quarterback, San Diego made it five division titles in six tries with a nine-two-three season. When honors were distributed, Paul Lowe was named Player of the Year, Earl Faison and Alworth were All League, and Hadl led the league in passing. But even that wasn't enough in the playoff, and once again the Chargers lost to Buffalo, this time by an embarrassing 23-0 score.

By the following season, the Chargers had lost some key specialists, Ladd (who said he did not want to play at San Diego) was traded to Houston, and four men—cornerbacks Dick Westmoreland and Jim Warren, offensive guard Ernie Park and tight end Dave Kacourek—were claimed by

Keith Lincoln (22), about to go all the way for a TD against Buffalo, 196

Miami, the expansion team. San Diego finished third.

One of the most mysterious races the Chargers displayed came in 1967 when, apparently stronger than ever, they won eight of their first ten games, tying one. They were getting superior work from Hadl at quarterback, Willie Frazier at tight end, rookie halfback Dick Post and, of course, Alworth and Gary Garrison. But that happened to be the year Oakland romped off with thirteen victories and only one defeat. After a key game in December, in which Oakland made believers of the San Diego crowd of 52,661 with a 41-21 triumph, the Chargers never won another game, losing to Miami, Houston and New York.

Something similar happened in 1968, and it began to appear that whatever gods had smiled on the Chargers in the first half-dozen years of the league's existence had abandoned them now. San Diego still was snapping at the heels of the leaders, Kansas City and Oakland, when December rolled around. When the Chargers beat Buffalo in a key game,

21-6, and Oakland also won, the standings were:

	W	L	To Play
Kansas City	9	2	3
Oakland	9	2	3
San Diego	8	3	3

But both the Chiefs and the Raiders won their remaining games, while San Diego fumbled away two of their remaining ones and the other two clubs ended in a tie, with the Chargers chugging in three games behind. Oakland defeated Kansas City for the division title, and then, of course, lost to the Jets in the championship game.

San Diego, as usual, shone in the statistics. Their fine ends, Alworth and Garrison, each scored ten touchdowns, Hadl led the quarterbacks in completions, yardage and touchdowns, Dick Post was fifth best rusher in the league and the team was second in points scored. But it still meant a third-place finish.

Still, Charger fans say, they have Sid Gillman, and if anybody can whip up a winning combination, he's the man. He has shown that in the past.

Miami's Larry Csonka (39) tears through the middle of a Charger line in 1968. Csonka is considered a valuable hope for the future

15... ■ ■ ■ THE MIAMI DOLPHINS

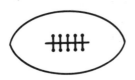

After performing for six years with two four-club divisions, the American League made its first expansion for the 1966 season when it tapped the Miami Dolphins as its fifth Eastern Division team and stocked it with manpower. To be sure, the manpower has been less than earth-shaking, but after its first year in last-place, the Dolphins climbed to fourth in 1967, to third in 1968 and each year improved just a little.

It was quite a gamble to place a pro team in Miami, for earlier efforts to introduce the game in that city had been failures. In 1946, a man named Harvey Hester, of Atlanta, Georgia, brought an All America Conference team called the Seahawks into Miami. The team had to play on Monday nights in order not to conflict with high school or college games, and all seven contests were played in driving rain. Two games had to be postponed because of hurricanes. The franchise lasted one year, in a bucket of red ink, before the Seahawks jumped to Baltimore.

Then, when the American League was being organized in 1959, Ralph Wilson, at the behest of Lamar Hunt, cased Miami for the new league, but found that the Orange Bowl would not permit professional teams to play there and since that was the only feasible site, Wilson took off for Buffalo, established the Bills and won three consecutive division titles in the mid-sixties.

The idea for the Miami franchise was born with a Minneapolis lawyer named Joe Robbie, who had attended college in South Dakota with Commissioner Joe Foss and who had later served in the state legislature with him. Robbie offered to establish a team in Miami and as one of his backers he won over another friend—comedian and television producer Danny Thomas. Robbie and Danny Thomas became major partners with seven other widely scattered partners completing the syndicate.

For a coach, the Dolphin management hired George Wilson, a one-time Chicago Bear player and assistant

Coach Wilson looks ahead to his fourth season.

captain of the offensive unit, while linebacker Tom Erlandson, from Denver, was captain of the defensive team.

Miami lost its first five games that year, even though George Wilson Jr., the coach's son, was showing some capability at quarterback, and Billy Joe and Joe Auer were doing yeoman service in rushing. By midseason, Cookie Gilchrist had joined the club and was displaying some of his ferocious line-lunging.

The three victories in 1966 increased to four in 1967 as Rick Norton, an All America from the University of Kentucky, took over at quarterback. His receivers were Jack Clancy from the University of Michigan, Paul Douglas of Louisiana State University and Howie Twilley of Tulsa. The Dolphins won one more game than the Patriots and edged them for fourth place.

But the real find for the Dolphins that year was their first pick in the original common draft when the two big leagues merged. They chose Bob Griese, the All America from Purdue, who finished the season as the American League's only rookie regular quarterback. Griese was named the club's most valuable player and best offensive back, finishing fifth in league passing statistics and giving hope to Miami fans for the future.

To complement Griese in 1968, Miami had a pair of power runners in rookie fullback Larry Csonka and third-year man Bronk Mitchell. The good receivers included Karl Noonan, Gene Milton, Twilley and Mitchell,

coach, who later was assistant coach and head coach of the Detroit Lions. When he was tapped for the Dolphin job, Wilson had been working as an assistant with the Washington Redskins. As talent procurer, the new club hired Joe Thomas, who had helped build the Minnesota Vikings into National League contention, and the publicity man was Charlie Callahan, the popular, hard-working Notre Dame publicist who had been with the Fighting Irish for twenty years.

Among the players the Dolphins plucked from the available list before their first season were some outstanding veterans. Gene Mingo and quarterback Dick Wood were acquired from the Oakland Raiders. Billy Joe, a well-traveled fullback, came from Buffalo, and Frank Jackson was flanker. The talented Dave Kocourek became the tight end and

The Dolphins' Jim Warren, right, tries for an interception against the Jets in an early '66 game

Despite the efforts of new star Bob Griese (12), the Dolphins dropped this one to the Chargers 24-0 for their seventh straight '67 loss

and when Jack Clancy recovered from knee troubles, experts thought the Dolphins would improve on their third place position achieved in 1968. Griese was the fourth best passer in the league with a 52.4 completions percentage and Noonan caught 58 passes for a 13.1 average gain and scored 11 touchdowns to tie for the league lead for pass receivers.

In three seasons, the Dolphins had achieved a semblance of respectability and their fans were showing their appreciation by turning out in greater and greater numbers. One day, the guessing was, they might even fill the 78,000-seat Orange Bowl—if Griese and his swift receivers stayed healthy.

16. ■ THE CINCINNATI BENGALS

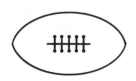

The tenth franchise awarded by the American Football League was given to the Cincinnati Bengals, owned by a syndicate headed by the fabled Paul Brown, one of the great coaches of history. His team took the field for the first time in 1968 and though, as anticipated, it wound up last in the Western Division, Paul Brown gave the other owners something to think about—for a short while—when the Bengals won two of their first three games. Cincinnati defeated the long-established Denver Broncos and Buffalo Bills and threw a scare into the powerful San Diego Chargers by holding them to a 10-10 halftime standoff. And at season's end, Brown had developed the Rookie of the Year in Paul Robinson of the University of Arizona, who led the league in yards gained, rushing; touchdowns, rushing, and longest touchdown run (87 yards against Oakland).

Brown was given full credit for the showing of his new team and he undoubtedly deserved it all. From his days as coach of Massillon (Ohio)

High School and Ohio State through his spectacular work in forming the Cleveland Browns of the All America Conference and dominating that rival of the National Football League, winning fifty-two of fifty-six games in four seasons, Brown was the complete football coach. He had forced the established league to take three of the old All America Conference teams into its ranks and then in 1963, he had been fired by Cleveland.

Brown always had his own methods of coaching, as the new Bengals discovered when they greeted him at summer camp in Wilmington, Ohio, in July, 1968. There were about 90 football players, including rookies and free agents and 31 castoffs picked up in the expansion draft of the American League. Paul Brown laid down his own law.

"There'll be no sugar coating or pampering of spoiled college kids," he said. "For the veterans, I don't know how you've been handled in the past or how big a name you have or how big car or how big a contract. Here

Coach Paul Brown, back in football after a five-year absence, was instrumental in developing the new Cincinnati team (1968)

it's meaningless. The only thing that counts here is your dedication to the game. You run on your own gas. It comes from within you.

"House rules: Rules are made for everybody so we can live together happily. It's a long, hard war. You have to go to every meal at training table. There will be a fifty-dollar fine for missing a meal without an excuse. We're going to live this thing together. I'm going to be there and I'm not going to ask you to do anything I'm not doing myself. I ask you to wear a sport shirt to dinner. At the table keep the meals enjoyable. Take your time. It's no place for pigs. Class always shows. Watch your language. Trips to Columbus and Cincinnati are out of bounds without permission . . .

"Home or away, we'll always be together the night before a game. We'll fight it right with you. We'll provide downtown hotel accommodations. We'll eat together, go to a movie together and room together. If you're a high-grade guy you will get somewhere. If you aren't you're in trouble.

"Nothing devastates a football team

Bengals' halfback Paul Robinson (18) plunges ahead against Miami. Cincinnati won the contest

Brown is the most respected coach in football.

like a selfish player. It's like cancer. The greatest back I ever had in my life was Marion Motley. You know why? The only statistic he ever knew was whether we won or lost. He was bigger and faster and the best blocker I ever had. But he was also the spirit of the team, completely unselfish . . .

"No smoking in public. If you must smoke go to your rooms. No smoking in the locker room or dining room. You're to go to your own room at 10:30 or thereabouts. At 11:00, turn out the lights. There will be nightly bedchecks. Maybe two or three a night if necessary. If you sneak out after bedcheck, the fine is five-hundred dollars. If you're late for practice

Robinson goes over the goal line for a TD against the Dolphins

Warren McVea (42) of the Bengals races to receive a TD
pass during the home opener, which they won 24-10

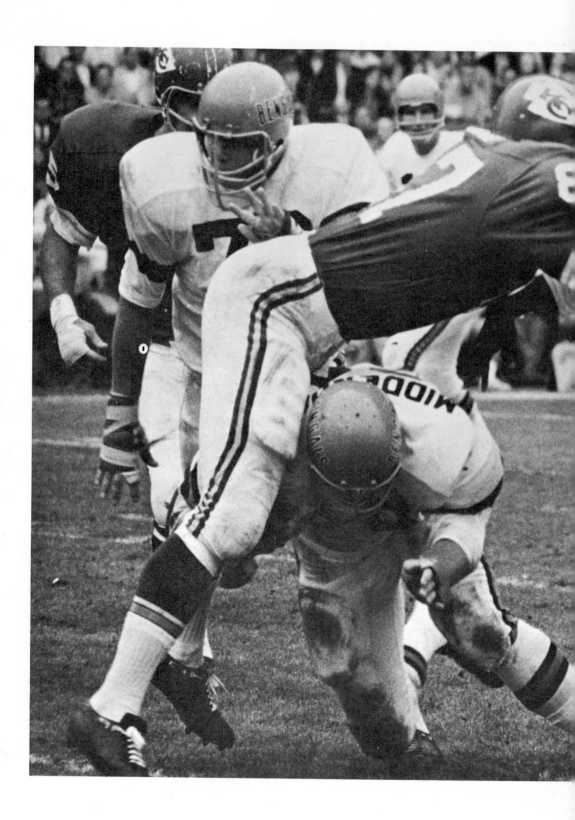

Robinson has the ball again—this time against K.C. The big halfback was the league leader in rushing

or a conference without permission, you'll also be fined. Hundred-dollar fine for missing a plane, plus having to pay your own way to the game. Automatic five-hundred dollar fine for losing your playbook.

"Now, maybe I've given you the wrong impression about these fines. But I think I had to hand out three fines in all the years I was with the Browns. It just didn't happen.

"Eleven times I've taken teams through to the championship game and I've got a pretty good idea of the kind of player it takes to get there. That's why I've taken the trouble to explain these things to you."

And the Bengals listened and performed well. With twenty-two rookies on the squad, seven of them started on offense and five on defense and what they lacked in experience they made up in drive and dedication to Paul Brown's philosophy of football.

By the end of the first season, the Bengals were a well-knit club, despite their last-place finish. Quarterback John Stofa, acquired from the Miami Dolphins, was sixth-best passer in the league. Behind league-leader Paul Robinson in rushing was Essex Johnson, a rookie. Rookie pass receiver, Bob Trumpy averaged 17.3 yards a reception. And kicker Dale Livingston, another rookie, had thirteen field goals and twenty conversions to place among the top ten scorers in the league.

With Paul Brown at the helm, it appeared that the Bengals were a team that would be heard from in the very near future.

17 THE NEW YORK TITANS-JETS

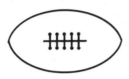

It all began for the New York Jets when they were the New York Titans and owned by the controversial broadcaster, bon vivant and football club owner, the late Harry Wismer.

Wismer, who had started as a spotter for Bill Stern at a Michigan State football broadcast back in the 'thirties, had become a legend in the sports business.

Having started in Detroit, he moved East and began broadcasting Washington Redskin games on his own. He was so successful that he drew notice as one of the Outstanding Men of the Year in the nation's capital. Wismer then bought a piece of the Redskins, made a substantial profit when he sold out, and continued to broadcast flamboyant football.

But most important, by the time the American League was started in 1959, the ebullient Wismer had bought the New York franchise.

There wasn't much that the other owners—all closed-corporation football men—trying to start a new league, could do about it. It was obvious that

if the league were to get off the ground, it needed a New York showcase, and Harry Wismer had the option.

He hired Steve Sebo as general manager, and Sammy Baugh, the famous Texas Christian and Redskin passer, as head coach.

In their first season, played at the broken-down old Polo Grounds already deserted by the New York baseball Giants in their flight to San Francisco, the Titans drew badly. But not according to Harry Wismer, who blithely doubled or trebled the actual attendance to make an "official attendance." The weekly head count became a newspaper joke, and one writer suggested that 12,000 of the announced attendance of 18,500 had "come disguised as empty seats."

But surprisingly, the Titan team wasn't too bad. With Al Dorow, who had been a back-up quarterback for the New York Giants, calling signals, and Don Maynard, another Giant castoff; rookie Bill Mathis, and veteran Art Powell operating efficiently,

Shea Stadium, December 29, 1968—the AFL Title game with Oakland. The Jets won, the crowd roared. They'd come a long way

Harry Wismer—the first man to see New York as an AFL town

Sonny Werblin who guided it all

Sammy Baugh was Wismer's first coach for the original Titans

Townsend Martin

Philip Iselin

Leon Hess

The foursome-owners of the Jets today

Helen Springborn

the team won seven and lost seven, good enough for second place in the Eastern division, behind the Houston Oilers.

In their second season, the Titans again finished seven-and-seven, this time being good only for third place, and Mathis led the league in rushing and Dorow threw more passes than any other quarterback. But Wismer had become disillusioned with coach Baugh and at season's end fired him in favor of Clyde (Bulldog) Turner, a former Chicago Bears great. There was a big hassle about the last year on Baugh's contract, which Wismer at first refused to recognize, but after much rumbling and grumbling, Baugh got his money and went back to his Texas ranch.

Under Turner, the Titans fell into the cellar, winning five and losing

New York's Bill Mathis (31) plunges over from a yard out to score against the Chargers. The Jets won 37-15

nine, and attendance dipped even further. That was the year the players' paychecks began not appearing on time and they even threatened a strike at one point. Later, Commissioner Joe Foss announced that the league was assuming the financial responsibilities of the Titans because of "ownership's failure to meet its obligations." Finally, Wismer was compelled to file for bankruptcy. A syndicate, headed by David A. (Sonny) Werblin, paid a million dollars for the franchise. The Titans were

out of business and the Jets were born. Poor Harry Wismer died in 1967.

Sonny Werblin came to football from the Music Corporation of America, in its day the largest talent agency in the world and later a potent force in the entertainment world. He was not the sole owner or even the majority stockholder of the Jets when his group bought in, but the others allowed Werblin to work things out. His notion was to bring entertainment values to the football field and one of

Jim Turner of the Jets kicks a field goal against Oakland during the 1968 AFL Championship game

Emerson Boozer (32) of the Jets gains against Boston, foiling the Patriot's attempt to clinch the Eastern Division championship (1966)

Paul Rochester (72) of the Jets about to bring down
Daryle Lamonica of Oakland in the 1968 AFL Title Game

his first moves was to hire Joe Cahill,
who had been sports information
man at West Point for years, as
public relations director. One of
his next moves was to hire Weeb Ewbank, who had been a successful
coach with the Baltimore Colts (and
twice beaten the New York Giants for
the championship) as his coach.

The team still wasn't terribly bad.
For three straight years under Ewbank it maintained the same won-
and-lost record—five-eight-one. One
year this meant last place; one year
it meant third and one year it meant
second. The players included Larry
Grantham, an All League linebacker;

Don Maynard, a good pass receiver
and fullback, and rusher Bill Mathis.
Matt Snell was drafted from Ohio
State and Werblin outbid the Giants
for him. The Jets also acquired the
colorful Wahoo McDaniel in a trade
with Denver and he added a little
juice to the proceedings.

In the new Shea Stadium, where
the baseball Mets were drawing
madly, the Jets began to do the same.
On opening day, 1964, a new American League record was set—45,497—
for the Denver game, and that was
broken for the San Diego game. Then,
in the key game of the year the Jets
played Buffalo at Shea Stadium. It

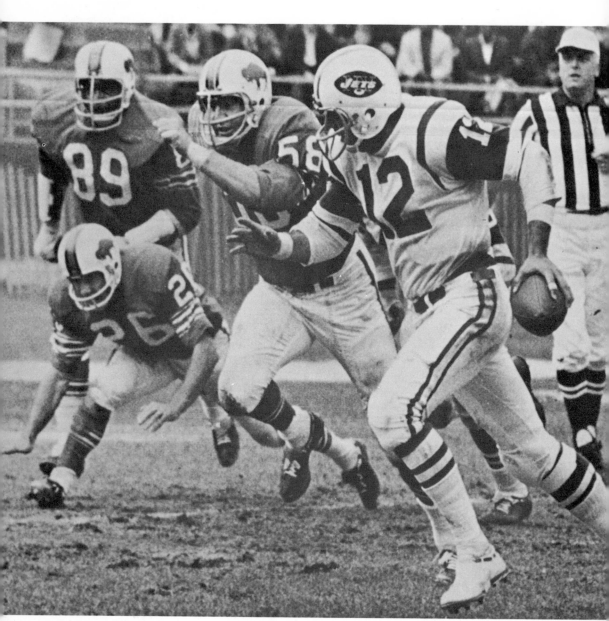

Jet QB Joe Namath bootlegs the ball against Buffalo

was a sell-out. The new club averaged 42,720 a game for seven games, the highest attendance average in the league. The Buffalo-Jet game proved that New York had become a two-team football city because on that same day the Giants were playing at Yankee Stadium, and they too drew the crowds. Obviously, New York had room for two teams.

Then came the year, 1965 and Joe Namath was signed, with the attendant publicity of his $400,000 bonus. The town went wild and the crowds grew bigger, even though the club still lost the division title by five games to the Buffalo Bills. By 1966, Namath was picking American League defenses apart, and he was finding splendid receivers among Matt Snell, Bill Mathis, George Sauer, Pete Lammons and Bake Turner. He still had his erratic afternoons, but it was apparent that he was where he belonged.

This despite the fact that his knees had been under surgery ever since he reported as a rookie. The right knee was operated on in January, 1965, before his first season. It had additional repairs the following December. Then before the 1968 season started, the left knee went under the doctor's knife. It didn't seem to bother him as he led the Jets to the Eastern division title, the league championship and

Namath again gets the pass off before being hit

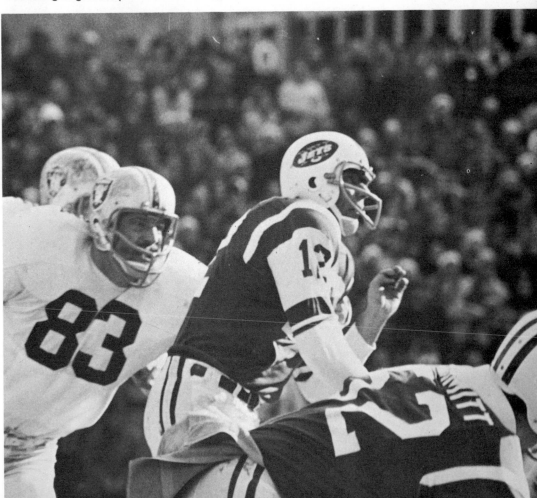

Weeb Ewbank watches George Sauer (83), take a Namath pass in the second period

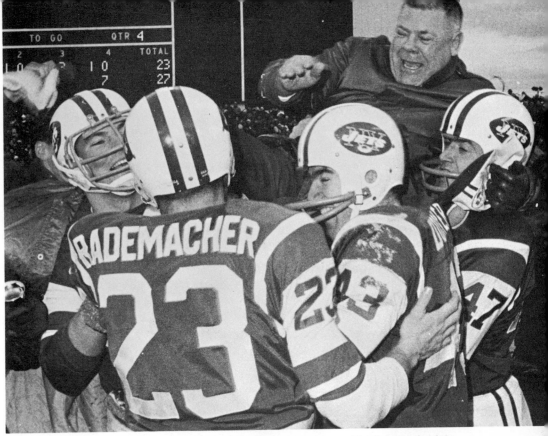

Coach Ewbank is carried off the field by excited players in end-game highjinks as the Jets took their first AFL championship on their way to the Super Bowl. December 29, 1968

Ewbank leaves the field, shaking hands with jubilant fans

the Super Bowl triumph. For those exploits, American League players voted him their oustanding player for the year and, of course, quarterback of the All-America League team.

But the fact remained. Joe Namath had come out of Beaver Falls, Pa. all the way from rookie to the Hickok Belt (Professional Athlete of the Year Award, 1968). In so doing he had brought the Jets a long way in four short years—and changed the face of the entire league.

"There are lots of stories about Namath," one player said, "about his long hair, his Fu Manchu mustache, about his white shoes, about his defiant attitude to reporters and photographers, but he is a ball player—all the way."

Namath himself gave credit to his front line—John Schmitt, Bob Talamini, Dave Herman, Randy Rasmussen, Winston Hill and Sam Walton—and his receivers—Sauer, Maynard, Pete Lammons, Snell and the rest.

18.■ ■ 1970–ONE BIG LEAGUE

In a marathon session in the spring of 1969, which ran thirty-five hours and forty-five minutes—and which saw covering newspapermen sleeping on the floor—the leagues decided to move the Baltimore Colts, the Cleveland Browns and the Pittsburgh Steelers into the A.F.L. That made both the National Football League and the new one even at thirteen clubs each. The way it was realigned was this:

AMERICAN CONFERENCE

Division One
Cincinnati Bengals
Cleveland Browns
(ex-N.F.L.)
Houston Oilers
Pittsburgh Steelers
(ex-N.F.L.)

Division Two
New York Jets
Baltimore Colts
(ex-N.F.L.)
Boston Patriots
Buffalo Bills
Miami Dolphins

Division Three
Denver Broncos
Kansas City Chiefs
Oakland Raiders
San Diego Chargers

In the National League, there remained the New York Giants, the Atlanta Falcons, the Chicago Bears, the Dallas Cowboys, the Detroit Lions, the Green Bay Packers, the Los Angeles Rams, the Minnesota Vikings, the New Orleans Saints, the Philadelphia Eagles, the St. Louis Cardinals, the San Francisco 49ers and the Washington Redskins.

The new alignment was exciting in some ways, for it placed the Colts and the Jets in the same division. It would put the 1969 Super Bowl rivals against each other twice a year, and there would be many football followers who would like that replay. Baltimore was a prestigious entry; so were the Browns of Cleveland. Pittsburgh, always an also-ran in the N.F.L., went under the influence of the Cleveland move.

Cleveland's switch came as something of a surprise because its owner, Art Modell, president of the National Football League and chief of the Cleveland team, had said and said that to shift into the A.F.L. would be disastrous, would, in fact, "emasculate the N.F.L."

Most reporters on the scene agreed that Commissioner Pete Rozelle leaned on the National League clubs to make the change. It was felt that Rozelle pointed a finger again and said: "O.K., YOU AND YOU AND YOU go the other league. Rozelle denied it. He said, in a formal statement, "After discussion with National Football League clubs, three of them who felt strongly about maintaining the identity built up between the A.F.L. and N.F.L. and who have deep faith in the future of the new American Conference agreed to make the move."

The clubs which decided (or were ordered) to move into the other league were well paid. They were to get over two million dollars each because of the lower "take" in A.F.L. cities.

It was, of course, the second league switch for Baltimore and Cleveland. Both clubs were founded in the old All America Conference in 1946 and switched to the National League in 1949.

Under the three division schedule, the A.F.L. clubs were to play a schedule of six intra-division home-and-home games, five intra-conference games and three cross-conference games. Each team was to play an eight-three-three schedule.

The name of the new revised league will be the National Football League with 2 Conferences—the American and the National.

A GLOSSARY

T Formation: This is the basic lineup on offense for all professional teams and most college and high school teams. The *quarterback* crouches behind the center and receives the ball. Behind him are the *halfback*, or running back, and the *fullback*, or plunging back. When the quarterback gets the ball, he either fades for a forward pass, or hands the ball to a runner, or, if something goes wrong, runs with it himself. The T offense looks like this:

```
O            O   O   O   O    O    O
SE          LT  LG   C   RG   RT   TE
                     O
                     QB
                                        O
                                        FB

        O           O
        HB          FB
```

The other designations, aside from the guards, tackles and center, are *split end, tight end* and *flanker back*, all of whom are eligible to catch passes. So are, of course, the two men in the backfield. Every action in pro football springs from this basic formation. How well the quarterback does depends on his linemen keeping the opposition out, his backs protecting him and his ends and backs running a preconceived pattern to confuse the other team.

Patterns: These vary. In the *square-out* pattern a receiver runs down field fakes to the inside and then runs toward the outside sideline to catch the pass. In the *fly* a receiver leaves the line of scrimmage at top speed deep into the secondary of the opposition—in a straight line. (Also called the *homer,* or *home run ball,* or *bomb.*) In a *pick,* a receiver moves in front of a defender in such a way as to prevent him from seeing another receiver crossing over. On a *swing,* or *flare* pass, the fullback or the running back moves laterally to take a pass from the quarterback. On a *screen,* offensive linemen let rushers through as the quarterback lofts a soft pass to a back, usually the fullback, who then runs behind the blocking screen set up by the linemen. The *safety valve* occurs when the quarterback as if to throw and his halfback and fullback assume blocking stances. But as blocking men. A *slant* is when a receiver, usually the flanker, cuts straight across at a 45-degree angle from his position, just in front of the opposing linebacker. (Also called a *look-in.*)

Blitzing: This is a defensive play in which the linebackers rush into the offensive backfield with the view of dumping the quarterback before the play gets started. (Also called *red-dogging.*)

Draw Play: In this, at which Joe Namath is a master, the quarterback drops back as if to throw and his halfback and fullback assure blocking stances. But as the quarterback passes the fullback, on the way to the throwing position, he slips the ball to the other man, who tries to find a hole in the line. (Sometimes the ball is given to the running back.)

Quarterback Sneak: Usually, when in very close scoring position, the offensive quarterback merely takes the ball from the center and dives underneath, hoping to find the last white line. On a variation of this, the T-formation quarterback will stick the ball on his hip, run wide to his right or left—after faking a handoff—and trot into the end zone—if he is good at it. This is called a keeper.

The Pocket: Where the quarterback should stay, in a small area formed by his blockers, before he throws the ball. Unless he is a *scrambler,* meaning he runs hither and yon until one of his receivers gets clear—if the other side doesn't reach him first. In that case, he is forced to *eat the ball,* a state of action in which he cannot find a man to throw to, and in which he is subdued by a host of tacklers. Or, if he is able, he can *throw the ball away,* or *ground it,* a tactic which is against the rules but is almost never called.

Game Plan: This is supposed to be the secret of the whole bustling world of pro football. Nobody knows exactly what it means, because if a team gets behind by two touchdowns in the first period, the game plan has to go out the window. In that case, it's *catch-up* football, and in that case, a team usually loses by more than it was expected to.

Unnecessary Roughness: This is what happens when you punch a man—who has been holding you all afternoon illegally—and you get caught.

STATISTICS

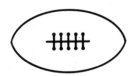

PLAYER OF THE YEAR	ROOKIE OF THE YEAR
1960...Abner Haynes, Dallas	1960...Abner Haynes, Dallas
1961...George Blanda, Houston	1961...Earl Faison, San Diego
1962...Len Dawson, Kansas City	1962...Curtis McClinton, Kansas City
1963...Clem Daniels, Oakland	1963...Billy Joe, Denver
1964...Gino Cappelletti, Boston	1964...Matt Snell, New York
1965...Paul Lowe, San Diego	1965...Joe Namath, New York
1966...Jim Nance, Boston	1966...Bob Burnett, Buffalo
1967...Daryle Lamonica, Oakland	1967...George Webster, Houston
1968...Joe Namath, New York	1968...Paul Robinson, Cincinnati

CONTINUED

LEAGUE ALL STAR TEAMS
1960–1968

1960

OFFENSE

E...Bill Groman, Houston
E...Lionel Taylor, Denver
T...Rich Michael, Houston
T...Ron Mix, Los Angeles
G...Billy Krisher, Dallas
G...Bob Mischak, New York
C...Jim Otto, Oakland
QB...Jack Kemp, Los Angeles
HB...Abner Haynes, Dallas
HB...Paul Lowe, Los Angeles
FB...Dave Smith, Houston

DEFENSE

E...LaVerne Torczon, Buffalo
E...Mel Branch, Dallas
T...Bud McFadin, Denver
T...Volney Peters, Los Angeles
LB...Archie Matsos, Buffalo
LB...Sherrill Headrick, Dallas
LB...Tom Addison, Boston
B...Richie McCabe, Buffalo
B...Dick Harris, Los Angeles
B...Ross O'Hanley, Boston
B...Austin Gonsoulin, Denver

* The keys to positions are B: Running Back. E: End. TE: Tight End. SE: Split End. T: Tackle. G: Guard. C: Center. QB: Quarterback. HB (or Running): Halfback. FB (or Plowing): Fullback. MLB: Middle Line Backer. OLB: Outside Linebacker. CB: Cornerback. S: Safety Man. P: Punter. K: Field Goal Kicker.

1961

OFFENSE

E...Lionel Taylor, Denver
E...Charley Hennigan, Houston
T...Ron Mix, San Diego
T...Al Jamison, Houston
G...Bob Mischak, New York
G...Charles Leo, Boston
C...Jim Otto, Oakland
QB...George Blanda, Houston
HB...Abner Haynes, Dallas
HB...Billy Cannon, Houston
FB...Billy Mathis, New York

DEFENSE

E...Earl Faison, San Diego
E...Don Floyd, Houston
T...Bud McFadin, Denver
T...Chuck McMurtry, Buffalo
LB...Sherrill Headrick, Dallas
LB...Archie Matsos, Buffalo
LB...Chuck Allen, San Diego
B...Tony Banfield, Houston
B...Dick Harris, San Diego
B...Dave Webster, Dallas
B...Charles McNeil, San Diego

1962

OFFENSE

TE...Dave Kocourek, San Diego
FL...Chris Burford, Dallas
SE...Charley Hennigan, Houston
T...Eldon Danenhauer, Denver
T...Jim Tyrer, Dallas
G...Bob Talamini, Houston
G...Ron Mix, San Diego
C...Jim Otto, Oakland
QB...Len Dawson, Dallas
HB...Abner Haynes, Dallas
FB...Cookie Gilchrist, Buffalo

DEFENSE

E...Don Floyd, Houston
E...Mel Branch, Dallas
T...Bud McFadin, Denver
T...Jerry Mays, Dallas
CLB...Larry Grantham, New York
CLB...E. J. Holub, Dallas
MLB...Sherrill Headrick, Dallas
CB...Tony Banfield, Houston
CB...Fred Williamson, Oakland
S...Austin Gonsoulin, Denver
S...Bob Zeman, Denver

1963

OFFENSE

TE...Fred Arbanas, Kansas City
SE...Art Powell, Oakland
FL...Lance Alworth, San Diego
T...Ron Mix, San Diego
T...Jim Tyrer, Kansas City
G...Billy Shaw, Buffalo
G...Bob Talamini, Houston
C...Jim Otto, Oakland
QB...Tobin Rote, San Diego
HB...Clem Daniels, Oakland
FB...Keith Lincoln, San Diego

DEFENSE

E...Larry Eisenhauer, Boston
E...Earl Faison, San Diego
T...Tom Sestak, Buffalo
T...Houston Antwine, Boston
MLB...Arch Matsos, Oakland
CLB...E. J. Holub, Kansas City
CLB...Tom Addison, Boston
CB...Dave Grayson, Kansas City
CB...Fred Williamson, Oakland
S...Fred Glick, Houston
S...Austin Gonsoulin, Denver

1964

OFFENSE

TE...Fred Arbanas, Kansas City
SE...Art Powell, Oakland
SE...Charley Hennigan, Houston
T...Ron Mix, San Diego
T...Jim Tyrer, Kansas City
G...Billy Shaw, Buffalo
G...Bob Talamini, Houston
C...Jim Otto, Oakland
GB...Babe Parilli, Boston
FL...Lance Alworth, San Diego
HB...Keith Lincoln, San Diego
FB...Cookie Gilchrist, Buffalo

DEFENSE

E...Earl Faison, San Diego
E...Larry Eisenhauer, Boston
T...Tom Sestak, Buffalo
T...Jerry Mays, Kansas City
MLB...Nick Buoniconti, Boston
CLB...Tom Addison, Boston
CLB...Larry Grantham, New York
CB...Willie Brown, Denver
CB...Dave Grayson, Kansas City
S...Fred Glick, Houston
S...Dainard Paulson, New York

1965

OFFENSE

TE...Willie Frazier, Houston
SE...Art Powell, Oakland
SE...Lionel Taylor, Denver
T...Jim Tyrer, Kansas City
T...Eldon Danenhauer, Denver
G...Billy Shaw, Buffalo
G...Bob Talamini, Houston
C...Jim Otto, Oakland
QB...Jack Kemp, Buffalo
FL...Lance Alworth, San Diego
HB...Paul Lowe, San Diego
FB...Cookie Gilchrist, Denver
K...Pete Gogolak, Buffalo
P...Curley Johnson, New York

DEFENSE

E...Earl Faison, San Diego
E...Jerry Mays, Kansas City
T...Tom Sestak, Buffalo
T...Ernie Ladd, San Diego
MLB...Nick Buoniconti, Boston
OLB...Mike Stratton, Buffalo
OLB...Bobby Bell, Kansas City
CB...Dave Grayson, Oakland
CB...George Byrd, Buffalo
S...George Saimes, Buffalo
S...John Robinson, Kansas City

1966

OFFENSE

TE...Fred Arbanas, Kansas City
SE...Art Powell, Oakland
T...Jim Tyrer, Kansas City
T...Sherman Plunkett, New York
G...Billy Shaw, Buffalo
G...Bob Talamini, Houston
C...Jim Otto, Oakland
QB...Len Dawson, Kansas City
FL...Lance Alworth, San Diego
HB...Clem Daniels, Oakland
FB...Jim Nance, Boston
K...Gino Cappelletti, Boston
P...Bob Scarpitto, Denver

DEFENSE

E...Jerry Mays, Kansas City
E...Larry Eisenhauer, Boston
T...Houston Antwine, Boston
T...Buck Buchanan, Kansas City
MLB...Nick Buoniconti, Boston
OLB...Bobby Bell, Kansas City
OLB...Mike Stratton, Buffalo
CB...Dave Grayson, Oakland
CB...George Byrd, Buffalo
S...John Robinson, Kansas City
S...George Saimes, Buffalo

1967

OFFENSE

TE...Willie Frazier, San Diego
SE...George Sauer, New York
T...Walt Suggs, Houston
T...Jim Tyrer, Kansas City
G...Bob Talamini, Houston
G...Gene Upshaw, Oakland
C...Jim Otto, Oakland
QB...Daryle Lamonica, Oakland
FL...Lance Elworth, San Diego
HB...Mike Garrett, Kansas City
FB...Hewritt Dixon, Oakland
K...George Blanda, Oakland
P...Bob Scarpitto, Denver

DEFENSE

E...Ben Davidson, Oakland
E...Jerry Mays, Kansas City
T...Tom Keating, Oakland
T...Buck Buchanan, Kansas City
MLB...Nick Buoniconti, Boston
OLB...George Webster, Houston
OLB...Bobby Bell, Kansas City
CB...Miller Farr, Houston
CB...Ken McCloughan, Oakland
S...George Saimes, Buffalo
S...Kenny Graham, San Diego

1968

OFFENSE

TE...Alvin Reed, Houston
SE...George Sauer, New York
T...Ron Mix, San Diego
T...Walt Suggs, Houston
G...Gene Upshaw, Oakland
G...Walt Sweeney, San Diego
C...Jim Otto, Oakland
QB...Joe Namath, New York
HB...Paul Robinson, Cincinnati
FB...Hewritt Dixon, Oakland
K...Jan Stenerud, Kansas City
P...Jerrel Wilson, Kansas City

DEFENSE

E...Gerry Philbin, New York
E...Jerry Mays, Kansas City
T...Dan Birdwell, Oakland
T...Houston Antwine, Boston
MLB...Nick Buoniconti, Boston
OLB...George Webster, Houston
OLB...Bobby Bell, Kansas City
CB...Miller Farr, Houston
CB...Willie Brown, Oakland
S...Johnny Robinson, Kansas City
S...Kenny Graham, San Diego

THE COACHES, BY TEAM

BOSTON
1960-61 Lou Saban*
1961-68 Mike Holovak
1969 Clive Rush

BUFFALO
1960-61 Buster Ramsey
1962-68 Joe Collier
1969 John Rauch

CINCINNATI
1968-69 Paul Brown

DENVER
1960-61 Frank Filchock
1962-64 Jack Faulkner*

1964-66 Mac Speedie*
1966 Ray Malavasi
1967-69 Lou Saban

HOUSTON
1960-61 Lou Rymkus*
1961-69 Wally Lemm
1962-63 Frank Ivy
1964 Sammy Baugh
1965 Hugh Taylor
1966 Wally Lemm

KANSAS CITY†
1960-69 Hank Stram

MIAMI
1966-69 George Wilson

NEW YORK
1960-61 Sammy Baugh
1962 Clyde Turner
1963-69 Weeb Ewbank

OAKLAND
1960-61 Eddie Erdelatz*
1961-62 Marty Feldman*
1962 William Conkright
1963-65 Al Davis
1966-68 John Rauch
1969 John Madden

SAN DIEGO*†
1960-69 Sid Gilman

* replaced before the end of his final season.
† Kansas City franchise located in Dallas, 1960-1962.
*† San Diego franchise located in Los Angeles, 1960.

FINAL STANDINGS

1960

EASTERN DIVISION

Team	W	L	T	Pts. For	Pts. Against	Pct.
Houston	10	4	0	379	285	.714
New York	7	7	0	382	399	.500
Buffalo	5	8	1	296	303	.385
Boston	5	9	0	286	349	.357

WESTERN DIVISION

Team	W	L	T	Pts. For	Pts. Against	Pct.
Los Angeles	10	4	0	373	336	.714
Dallas	8	6	0	362	253	.571
Oakland	6	8	0	319	388	.429
Denver	4	9	1	309	393	.308

Championship Game: Houston 24, Los Angeles 16.

1961

EASTERN DIVISION

Team	W	L	T	Pts. For	Pts. Against	Pct.
Houston	10	3	1	513	242	.769
Boston	9	4	1	413	313	.692
New York	7	7	0	301	390	.580
Buffalo	6	8	0	294	342	.429

WESTERN DIVISION

Team	W	L	T	Pts. For	Pts. Against	Pct.
San Diego	12	2	0	396	219	.857
Dallas	6	8	0	334	343	.429
Denver	3	11	0	251	432	.214
Oakland	2	12	0	237	458	.143

Championship Game: Houston 10, San Diego 3.

1962

EASTERN DIVISION

Team	W	L	T	Pts. For	Pts. Against	Pct.
Houston	11	3	0	387	270	.786
Boston	9	4	1	346	295	.692
Buffalo	7	6	1	309	272	.538
New York	5	9	0	278	423	.357

WESTERN DIVISION

Team	W	L	T	Pts. For	Pts. Against	Pct.
Dallas	11	3	0	389	233	.786
Denver	7	7	0	353	334	.500
San Diego	4	10	0	314	392	.286
Oakland	1	13	0	213	370	.071

Championship Game: Dallas 20, Houston 17.

1963

EASTERN DIVISION

Team	W	L	T	Pts. For	Pts. Against	Pct.
Boston	7	6	1	317	257	.538
Buffalo	7	6	1	304	291	.538
Houston	6	8	0	302	372	.428
New York	5	8	1	249	399	.384

WESTERN DIVISION

Team	W	L	T	Pts. For	Pts. Against	Pct.
San Diego	11	3	0	399	256	.785
Oakland	10	4	0	363	288	.714
Kansas City	5	7	2	347	263	.416
Denver	2	11	1	301	473	.153

Championship Game: San Diego 51, Boston 10.

1964

EASTERN DIVISION

Team	W	L	T	Pts. For	Pts. Against	Pct.
Buffalo	12	2	0	400	242	.875
Boston	10	3	1	365	297	.769
New York	5	8	1	278	315	.385
Houston	4	10	0	310	355	.286

WESTERN DIVISION

Team	W	L	T	Pts. For	Pts. Against	Pct.
San Diego	8	5	1	341	300	.615
Kansas City	7	7	0	366	306	.500
Oakland	5	7	2	303	350	.417
Denver	2	11	1	240	438	.154

Championship Game: Buffalo 20, San Diego 7.

1965

EASTERN DIVISION

Team	W	L	T	Pts. For	Pts. Against	Pct.
Buffalo	10	3	1	313	226	.769
New York	5	8	1	285	303	.385
Boston	4	8	2	244	302	.333
Houston	4	10	0	298	429	.286

WESTERN DIVISION

Team	W	L	T	Pts. For	Pts. Against	Pct.
San Diego	9	2	3	340	227	.818
Oakland	8	5	1	298	239	.615
Kansas City	7	5	2	322	285	.583
Denver	4	10	0	303	392	.286

Championship Game: Buffalo 23, San Diego 0.

1966

EASTERN DIVISION

Team	W	L	T	Pts. For	Pts. Against	Pct.
Buffalo	9	4	1	358	255	.692
Boston	8	4	2	315	283	.667
New York	6	6	2	322	312	.500
Houston	3	11	0	335	396	.214
Miami	3	11	0	213	362	.214

WESTERN DIVISION

Team	W	L	T	Pts. For	Pts. Against	Pct.
Kansas City	11	2	1	448	276	.846
Oakland	8	5	1	315	288	.615
San Diego	7	6	1	335	284	.538
Denver	4	10	0	196	381	.286

Championship Game: Kansas City 31, Buffalo 7.

1967

EASTERN DIVISION

Team	W	L	T	Pts. For	Pts. Against	Pct.
Houston	9	4	1	258	199	.692
New York	8	5	1	371	329	.615
Buffalo	4	10	0	237	285	.286
Miami	4	10	0	219	407	.286
Boston	3	10	1	280	389	.231

WESTERN DIVISION

Team	W	L	T	Pts. For	Pts. Against	Pct.
Oakland	13	1	0	468	233	.929
Kansas City	9	5	0	408	254	.643
San Diego	8	5	1	360	352	.615
Denver	3	11	0	256	409	.214

Championship Game: Oakland 40, Houston 7.

1968

EASTERN DIVISION

Team	W	L	T	Pts. For	Pts. Against	Pct.
New York	11	3	0	419	280	.786
Houston	7	7	0	303	248	.500
Miami	5	8	1	276	355	.385
Boston	4	10	0	229	406	.286
Buffalo	1	12	1	199	367	.077

WESTERN DIVISION

Team	W	L	T	Pts. For	Pts. Against	Pct.
Oakland	13	2	0	494	239	.867
Kansas City	12	3	0	377	211	.800
San Diego	9	5	0	382	310	.643
Denver	5	9	0	255	404	.357
Cincinnati	3	11	0	215	329	.214

Championship Game: New York 27, Oakland 23.

RUSHING LEADER

		Yards Gained
1968	Paul Robinson, Cincinnati	1,023
1967	James Nance, Boston	1,216
1966	James Nance, Boston	1,458
1965	Paul Lowe, San Diego	1,121
1964	Carlton Gilchrist, Buffalo	981
1963	Clemon Daniels, Oakland	1,098
1962	Carlton Gilchrist, Buffalo	1,096
1961	William Cannon, Houston	948
1960	Abner Haynes, Dallas	875

SCORING		TD	FG	PAT	Total Pts.
1968	Robert Turner, New York	0	43	34	145
1967	George Blanda, Oakland	0	56	20	116
1966	Gino Cappelletti, Boston	6	35	16	119
1965	Gino Cappelletti, Boston	9	27	17	132
1964	Gino Cappelletti, Boston	7	25	37	155
1963	Gino Cappettetti, Boston	2	22	35	113
1962	Eugene Mingo, Denver	4	27	32	137
1961	Gino Cappelletti, Boston	8	17	48	147
1960	Eugene Mingo, Denver	6	18	33	123

FORWARD PASSING		Atts.	Comp.	Yards
1968	Len Dawson, Kansas City	224	131	2,109
1967	Daryle Lamonica, Oakland	425	220	3,228
1966	Len Dawson, Kansas City	284	159	2,527
1965	John Hadl, San Diego	348	174	2,789
1964	Len Dawson, Kansas City	354	199	2,879
1963	Tobin Rote, San Diego	287	170	2,510
1962	Len Dawson, Dallas	310	189	2,759
1961	George Blanda, Houston	362	187	3,330
1960	Jack Kemp, Los Angeles	407	211	3,108

PASS RECEIVING		Completions	Yards
1968	Lance Alworth, San Diego	68	1,312
1967	George Sauer, New York	75	1,189
1966	Lance Alworth, San Diego	73	1,383
1965	Lionel Taylor, Denver	85	1,131
1964	Charles Hennigan, Houston	101	1,561
1963	Lionel Taylor, Denver	78	1,101
1962	Lionel Taylor, Denver	77	908
1961	Lionel Taylor, Denver	100	1,176
1960	Lionel Taylor, Denver	92	1,235

FIELD GOALS		
1968	Robert Turner, New York	34
1967	Jan Stenerud, Kansas City	21
1966	Michael Mercer, Oakland—Kansas City	21
1965	Peter Gogolak, Buffalo	28
1964	Gino Cappelletti, Boston	25
1963	Gino Cappelletti, Boston	22
1962	Eugene Mingo, Denver	27
1961	Gino Cappelletti, Boston	17
1960	Eugene Mingo, Denver	18

PUNTING		Punts	Average Yards Per Kick
1968	Jerrell Wilson, Kansas City	63	45.1
1967	Robert Scarpitto, Denver	105	44.9
1966	Robert Scarpitto, Denver	76	45.8
1965	Jerrel Wilson, Kansas City	68	46.1
1964	James Fraser, Denver	70	44.6
1963	James Fraser, Denver	78	45.8
1962	James Fraser, Denver	54	44.4
1961	William Atkins, Buffalo	84	45.0
1960	Paul Maguire, Los Angeles	43	40.5

INTERCEPTION LEADER		Number
1968	David Grayson, Oakland	10
1967	Miller Farr, Houston	10
1966	John Robinson, Kansas City	10
1965	Wilmer Hicks, Houston	9
1964	Dainard Paulson, New York	12
1963	Gary Glick, Houston	12
1962	Leon Riley, New York	11
1961	William Atkins, Buffalo	10
1960	Austin Gonsalia, Denver	11

ALL-TIME LEAGUE STATISTICS

ALL-TIME RUSHERS (Yards Gained)	Years In League	Attempts	Yards	Touchdowns
Clem Daniels, Dallas, Oakland	8	1134	5101	30
Paul Lowe, Los Angeles, San Diego	8	1016	4962	39
Abner Haynes, Dallas, Kansas City, Denver	8	1036	4630	46
Cookie Gilchrist, Buffalo Denver, Miami	6	1010	4293	37
Jim Nance, Boston	4	856	3588	27
Keith Lincoln, San Diego	8	758	3383	19
Wray Carlton, Buffalo	8	819	3368	29
Matt Snell, New York	5	802	3309	19
Charley Tolar, Houston	7	907	3277	21
Bill Mathis, New York	9	948	3234	33

ACTIVE RUSHERS NOT IN TOP ALL-TIME 10

Curt McClinton, Kansas City	7	762	3124	18
Larry Garron, Boston	9	759	2981	14
Mike Garrett, Kansas City	3	547	2452	18
Billy Cannon, Oakland	9	601	2449	17
Hoyle Granger, Houston	3	494	2430	14
Billy Joe, New York	6	539	2010	15
Hewritt Dixon, Oakland	6	468	1831	14
Wendell Hayes, Kansas City	4	405	1538	14
Dick Post, San Diego	2	312	1421	10
Sid Blanks, Houston	5	345	1366	7

ALL-TIME PASSERS

	Yrs.	Atts.	Comp.	Pct.	TDs	Int.	Avg. Gain
Len Dawson, Dallas, Kansas City	7	2186	1237	56.6	173	104	8.04
Joe Namath, New York	4	1682	841	50.0	78	87	7.58
John Hadl, San Diego	7	2188	1081	49.4	133	134	7.67
Tom Flores, Oakland, Buffalo	8	1708	835	48.9	92	92	6.97
Daryl Lamonica, Buffalo, Oakland	6	1194	576	48.2	71	58	7.51
Babe Parilli, Oakland, Boston, New York	9	2655	1256	47.3	142	151	6.84
George Blanda, Houston, Oakland	9	2871	1392	48.5	174	194	6.95
Jack Kemp, San Diego, Buffalo	8	2711	1258	46.4	101	159	7.06
Frank Tripucka, Denver	4	1277	662	51.8	51	85	6.01
Cotton Davidson, Dallas, Oakland	8	1686	742	44.0	73	102	6.79

ALL-TIME RECEIVERS
(Based on Number of Receptions)

	Years	Receptions	Yards	Touchdowns
Lionel Taylor, Denver, Houston	9	567	7195	45
Don Maynard, New York	9	498	9349	78
Art Powell, New York, Oakland	8	478	8015	81
Charley Hennigan, Houston	7	410	6823	51
Lance Alworth, San Diego	7	394	7973	73
Chris Burford, Dallas, Kansas City	8	391	5505	55
Elbert Dubenion, Buffalo	9	294	5294	35
Gino Cappelletti, Boston	9	291	4568	42
Abner Haynes, Dallas, Kansas City, Denver	8	287	3535	20
Jim Colclough, Boston	9	283	5001	39

ACTIVE PASS RECEIVERS NOT IN TOP ALL-TIME 10

Dave Kocourek, Oakland	9	249	4090	24
George Sauer, New York	4	234	3712	16
Billy Cannon, Oakland	9	208	3269	43
Art Graham, Boston	6	199	3107	20
Hewritt Dixon, Oakland	6	199	2337	14
Larry Garron, Boston	9	185	2502	26
Bake Turner, New York	6	180	2781	19
Charlie Frazier, Houston	7	177	3037	22
Fred Arbanas, Kansas City	7	174	2735	33

ALL-TIME SCORERS

	Years	TDs	PATs	FGs	Points
Gino Cappelletti, Boston	9	42	312	156	1032
George Blanda, Houston, Oakland	9	4	411	132	831
Gene Mingo, Denver, Oakland, Miami	8	13	152	91	503
Art Powell, New York, Oakland	8	81	0	0	486
Jim Turner, New York	5	0	177	102	483
Don Maynard, New York	9	78	2	0	470
Lance Alworth, San Diego	7	75	2	0	452
Abner Haynes, Dallas, Kansas City, Denver	8	69	0	0	414
Mike Mercer, Oakland, Kansas City, Buffalo	6	0	180	69	387
Billy Cannon, Houston, Oakland	9	61	2	0	368

ACTIVE SCORERS NOT IN TOP ALL-TIME 10

Paul Lowe, Kansas City	8	46	0	0	276
Keith Lincoln, San Diego	8	40	16	5	271
Lionel Taylor, Houston	9	45	0	0	270
Bill Mathis, New York	9	41	6	0	252
Larry Garron, Boston	9	42	0	0	252
Jack Kemp, Buffalo	8	40	2	0	242
Jim Colclough, Boston	9	39	4	0	238
Jan Stenerud, Kansas City	2	0	84	51	237

ALL-TIME INTERCEPTORS

	Years	Number	Yards	Touchdowns
Jim Norton, Houston	9	45	592	1
Austin Gonsoulin, Denver	7	43	542	2
Dave Grayson, Dallas, Kansas City, Oakland	8	39	776	4
Bobby Hunt, Dallas, Kansas City, Cincinnati	7	38	689	1
Fred Williamson, Oakland, Kansas City	7	36	479	2
Johnny Robinson, Dallas, Kansas City	9	35	375	1
Freddie Glick, Houston	6	30	390	1
George Byrd, Buffalo	5	29	508	3
Ron Hall, Boston	7	29	476	1
Dick Harris, Los Angeles, San Diego	6	29	413	5
Bill Baird, New York	6	29	347	2
Dainard Paulson, New York	6	29	343	1
Willie West, Buffalo, Denver, New York, Miami	7	29	318	0

ACTIVE INTERCEPTORS NOT IN TOP ALL-TIME 10

Tom Janik, Buffalo	6	24	549	6
Willie Brown, Oakland	6	24	255	2
Nick Buoniconti, Boston	7	24	223	0
W. K. Hicks, Houston	5	23	421	0
Booker Edgerson, Buffalo	7	22	421	2
Warren Powers, Oakland	6	22	366	2
Dick Westmoreland, Miami	6	22	310	2
Kenny Graham, San Diego	5	21	365	3

INDEX

A

Adams, Bud   49-54, 93, 94, 100, (fig.) 98
Addison, Tommy   59, 60
Agajanian, Ben   52
All America Football Conference   48, 70
All Americans, Buffalo   70
Allen, Chuck   107
Alworth, Lance   75, 107, 108, 109
American Football League   47, 48, 49-54
American Professional Football League   45, 47, 70
Americans, Pittsburgh   47
Antwine, Houston   59
Arbanas, Fred   61
Atkinson, Al   31
Atkinson, George   20
Auer, Joe   112

B

Baird, Bill   31
Baker, Ralph   22, 31
Ball, Sam   31
Baltimore Colts (see Colts, Baltimore)
Banaszak, Pete   20
Banfield, Tony   101
Bass, Glenn   75, 85
Baugh, Sammy   102, (figs.) 51, 95, 126
Bears, Chicago   45, 47, 48
Beathard, Pete   102, (fig.) 62
Bell, Bert   50
Bell, Bobby   61, (fig.) 65
Bengals, Cincinnati   18, 47, 54, 115-122
Beverly, Randy   26, 27, 31, 34
Bierne, Jim   102
Biggs, Earl   31
Biggs, Verlon   22, 31
Biletnikoff, Fred   19, 20, 82, 85, (figs.) 83, 84
Bills, Buffalo   17, 70-77, 82, 88, 90, 108, 109, 111, 115, 133
Bisons, Buffalo   65, 131
Blanda, George   19, 20, 52, 85, 93 97, 100, 101, 102, (figs.) 96, 100
Blanks, Sid   102
Boozer, Emerson   31, (figs.) 33, 130
Boston Patriots (see Patriots, Boston)
Boston Shamrocks (see Shamrocks, Boston)
Boyd, Bob   24, 31
Boyer, E. William   49
Braase, Ordell   24, 31
Branch, Mel   61
Breen, John   93
Brinkley, Charlie   44
Briscoe, Marlin   92
Broncos, Denver   17, 51, 75, 76, 87-92, 115
Brooker, Tom   52
Brooklyn Dodgers (see Dodgers, Brooklyn)
Brooklyn Tigers (see Tigers, Brooklyn)
Brown, Paul   115, (figs.) 116, 118
Browns, Cleveland   23, 48, 93
Bryant, Paul (Bear)   39, 41

Buchanan, Buck   61
Buffalo All Americans (see All Americans, Buffalo)
Buffalo Bills (see Bills, Buffalo)
Buffalo Bisons (see Bisons, Buffalo)
Bulldogs, Canton   45
Bulldogs, Los Angeles   47
Bulldogs, New York   48
Buoniconti, Nick   60
Burford, Chris   61
Burnett, Bobby   76, (fig.) 75
Burton, Ron   59

C

Callahan, Charlie   112
Campbell, Woodie   102
Cannon, Billy   52, 94, 97, 101, (fig.) 98
Canton Bulldogs (see Bulldogs, Canton)
Cappelletti, Gino   56, 59, (fig.) 55
Cardinals, Chicago   48, 49
Carmichael, Al   88
Carr, Joe   44, 45
Carson, Johnny   93
Chargers, Los Angeles   97, 103
Chargers, San Diego   17, 18, 52, 59, 74, 75, 76, 78, 82, 90, 100, 103-110, 115
Chicago Bears (see Bears, Chicago)
Chicago Cardinals (see Cardinals, Chicago)
Chicago Hornets (see Hornets, Chicago)
Chicago Rockets (see Rockets, Chicago)
Chiefs, Kansas City   17, 18, 61-69, 76, 85, 109
Cincinnati Bengals (see Bengals, Cincinnati)
Clancy, Jack   112
Cleveland Browns (see Browns, Cleveland)
Cleveland Rams (see Rams, Cleveland)
Collier, Joel   76, (fig.) 73
Colts, Baltimore   23, 24, 26-36, 48, (figs.) 27, 28, 29, 30, 31, 32, 33, 35
Conkweight, Red   80
Cowboys, Dallas   23, 61, 93, 100, 101, 107
Crabtree, Eric   87
Crockett, Bobby   76
Crump, Harry   (fig.) 60
Csonka, Larry   112, (fig.) 110
Curry, Bill   31
Curtis, Mike   24, 31, (fig.) 28

D

Dallas Cowboys (see Cowboys, Dallas)
Dallas Texans (see Texans, Dallas)
D'Amato, Mike   (fig.) 35
Daniels, Clem   80, 82
Davidson, Ben   85, (fig.) 22
Davidson, Cotton   82
Davis, Al   53, 54, 80, 82, 85, 105, (fig.) 80
Dawson, Len   17, 52, 61, 65, 69, (figs.) 21, 64

153

Day, Tom   75
Denson, Al   87
Denver Broncos (see Broncos, Denver)
Dewveall, Williard   100
Dixon, Hewritt   85, (figs.) 81, 84
Dodgers, Brooklyn   48
Dolphins, Miami   18, 102, 109, 111-114
Dorais, Gus   44
Dorow, Al   123, 127
Douglas, Paul   112
Dovell, Whitey   92
Draper, Phil   42
Dubenion, Elbert   72, 75, (fig.) 76
Dunaway, Jim   75

E

Eisenhauer, Larry   59, 60
Elliott, John   31
Enis, Hunter   92
Erdelatz, Eddie   78, (fig.) 85
Erlandson, Tom   112
Ewbank, Weeb   131, (figs.) 24, 25, 35,
    38, 122, 135

F

Faison, Earl   107, 108
Farr, Miller   102
Faulkner, Jack   90, 92, 105
Feldman, Marty   78, 79
Filchock, Frank   87, 90, (fig.) 51
Flores, Tom   78, 82, 85
Floyd, Don   101
Ford, Garrett   92
Ford, Whitey   34
49ers, San Francisco   48
Foss, Joe   50, 52, 82, 128, (fig.) 53
Frazier, Willie   109

G

Gallagher, Dick   70
Garrett, Mike   61, 65, 69, (figs.) 65,
    66
Garrison, Gary   109
Garron, Larry   (fig.) 58
Gaubatz, Dennis   24, 31
Giants, New York   46, 47, 48, 54
Gilchrist, Cookie   59, 73, 75, 87, 92,
    112, (fig.) 71
Gillman, Sid   103, 107, 109, (figs.)
    103, 105
Glick, Fred   102
Gogolak, Pete   54, 74, 75, 76, (fig.) 71
Graham, Art   56, (fig.) 58
Grange, 'Red'   45, 46, 47
Granger, Hoyle   102
Grantham, Larry   31, 34, 131
Grayson, Dave   61, (fig.) 19
Green Bay Packers (see Packers, Green
    Bay)
Griese, Bob   112, 114, (fig.) 114
Griffing, Dean   87, 90
Groman, Bill   52, 93

H

Hadl, John   75, 107, 108, 109, (fig.)
    107
Hagberg, Roger   (fig.) 84
Haik, Mac   102
Halas, George   45, 49, 50
Harris, Dick   106, 107
Hay, Ralph   45
Hayes, Wendell   87
Haynes, Abner   52, 62, 87, 92
Headrick, Sherrill   61
Heffelfinger, Pudge   42
Hennigan, Charlie   93, 101, 102
Herman, Dave   31, 136
Hester, Harvey   111
Heston, Billy   44
Hill, Jerry   24, 26, 31, 33, 34
Hill, Winston   31, 32, 33, 136
Hilton, Barron   49, 52, 103, 106
Holmes, Bob   61
Holmes, Pat   102
Holovak, Mike   56, 60, (fig.) 56
Holub, E. J.   61
Hope, Bob   38
Hornets, Chicago   48
Horton, Don   107
Houston, Kenny   102
Houston Oilers (see Oilers, Houston)
Howsam, Bob   49, 87
Howsam, Earl   87
Howsam, Lee   87
Hudson, Bill   107
Hudson, Jim   31, 33
Hunt, Lamar   49-54, 61, 62, 70, 111,
    (fig.) 50

I

Ivy, Pop   101, 102

J

Jackson, Frank   112
Jamison, Al   101
Jets, New York   17-22, 26-36, (figs.) 19,
    20, 21, 22, 27, 28, 29, 30, 31, 32, 33,
    35, 53, 60,76, 85, 102, 109, 123-136
Joe, Billy   87, 88, 112, (fig.) 88-89
Johnson, Essex   121
Johnson, Harvey   76
Johnson, Stone   62
Jones, Stan   92
Jurgenson, Sonny   35

K

Kacourek, Dave   107, 108, 112
Kansas City Chiefs (see Chiefs, Kansas
    City)
Keating, Tom   85
Kemp, Jack   60, 73, 74, 75, 100, 106,
    107, 108, (figs.) 74, 108
Klosterman, Don   105
Kunz, Calvin   90

L

Ladd, Ernie   102, 107, 108
Lammons, Pete   19, 31, 133, 136, *(fig.)*
    28
Lamonica, Daryle   18, 19, 20, 22, 74, 85,
    102, *(figs.)* 20, 83, 131
Larscheid, Jack   78
Leahy, Frank   105
LeClair, Jim   92
Lee, Jacky   93, 97
Lemm, Wally   95, 100, 101, 102
Lincoln, Keith   59, 106, 107, 108, *(figs.)*
    21, 109
Lindsay, John V.   41
Little, Floyd   87, 92
Livingston, Bob   121
Logan, Jerry   24, 31
Loll, Billy   78
Los Angeles Bulldogs *(see* Bulldogs,
    Los Angeles)
Los Angeles Chargers *(see* Chargers,
    Los Angeles)
Los Angeles Rams *(see* Rams, Los
    Angeles)
Lowe, Paul   52, 75, 106, 107, 108,
    (fig.) 104-105
Lusteg, Booth   76
Lyles, Len   24, 31
Lynch, Fran   92
Lyons, Leo   45

M

MacPherson, Dick   92
McCabe, Richie   70
McClinton, Curt   52, 69
McCloughan, Kent   85
McDaniel, Wahoo   131
McDole, Ron   75
McGee, Max   69
McLaughry, Tuss   44
McLean, Ken   76
McNeil, Charlie   107
McVea, Warren   *(fig.)* 119
Mack, Connie   44
Mackey, John   26, 31, 34
Malavasi, Ray   92, *(fig.)* 90
Mara, Timothy J.   46
Mathewson, Christy   44
Mathis, Bill   22, 32, 123, 127, 131, 133,
    (fig.) 101
Matsos, Archie   70
Matte, Tom   24, 26, 31, 33
Maynard, Don   19, 20, 22, 31, 32, 123,
    131, 136, *(fig.)* 65
Mays, Jerry   61
Miami Dolphins *(see* Dolphins, Miami)
Miami Seahawks *(see* Seahawks, Miami)
Michael, Rich   97, 102
Michaels, Lou   24, 25, 26, 34
Miller, Fred   24, 31
Milstead, Charlie   93
Milton, Gene   112

Mingo, Gene   87, 88, 112, *(fig.)* 86
Mitchell, Bronk   112
Mitchell, Tom   26, 27, 34
Mix, Ron   106
Moore, Zeke   *(fig.)* 99
Moran, Charlie   44
Morrall, Earl   23, 24, 25, 26, 31, 33,
    35, *(fig.)* 27
Motley, Marion   118

N

Namath, Joe   17, 18, 19, 20, 21, 25, 31,
    32, 33, 34, 37-41, 53, 60, 85, 102,
    133, 136, *(figs.)* 18, 22, 25, 29, 32,
    33, 35, 37-41, 132, 133
Nance, Jim   60, 65, *(fig.)* 57
National Football League   45, 47, 53-54
Neale, Earl (Greasy)   44
Neid, Frank   45
Nerv, Ron   107
New Orleans Saints *(see* Saints, New Orleans)
New York Bulldogs *(see* Bulldogs, New York)
New York Giants *(see* Giants, New York)
New York Jets *(see* Jets, New York)
New York Titans *(see* Titans, New York)
New York Yankees *(see* Yankees, New York)
Norton, Rick   112
Noonan, Karl   112, 114

O

Oakland Raiders *(see* Raiders, Oakland)
Oilers, Houston   17, 51, 52, 60, 61, 78,
    82, 85, 90, 92, 93-102, 106, 107, 109,
    127
Okeson, Walter   42
Orr, Jimmy   31, 33, 34
Otto, Gus   82
Otto, Jim   85

P

Packers, Green Bay   69, 85
Parilli, Babe   25, 56, 59, 78, *(fig.)* 55
Park, Ernie   108
Parker, Willie   102
Patriots, Boston   17, 50, 51, 55-60, 80,
    88, 90, 112
Peters, Volney   106
Philbin, Gerry   31, *(fig.)* 27
Phipps, Gerald   90, 92
Pierce, Bemus   42
Pierce, Hawey   42
Pitts, Frank   61
Pittsburgh Americans *(see* Americans,
    Pittsburgh)
Poe, Arthur   42
Post, Dick   109
Powell, Art   82, 85, 123
Powers, Charlie   107
Professional football, history of   42-48
Pyle, C. C.   46, 47

R

Raiders, Oakland   17-22, 78-86, 97, 102, 109, 124, 125, (figs.) 19, 20, 21, 22
Rams, Cleveland   47, 48
Rams, Los Angeles   23, 48
Ramsey, Buster   51, 70, 72
Rasmussen, Randy   66, 136
Rauch, John   82, (fig.) 80
Reed, Alvin   102
Ressler, Glenn   31
Richardson, Willie   31, 33, 34, (fig.) 30
Robbie, Joe   111
Robinson, John   61, (fig.) 62
Robinson, Paul   115, 121, (figs.) 117, 118, 121
Rochester, Paul   31, (fig.) 131
Rochester Tigers (see Tigers, Rochester)
Rockets, Chicago   48
Rockne, Knute   44
Rood, Alvin, (fig.) 62
Rote, Tobin   74
Rozelle, Pete   50, 54, 94
Rush, Clive   60
Rutigliano, Sam   92
Rymkus, Lou   94, 100, 102, (figs.) 94, 95

S

Saban, Lou   75, 76, 92, (figs.) 72, 88
Saints, New Orleans   54
Sample, John   19, 26, 31, 33, 34, (fig.) 30
San Diego Chargers (see Chargers, San Diego)
San Francisco 49ers (see 49ers, San Francisco)
Sauer, George   20, 22, 31, 32, 133, 136
Schlinkman, Walt   102
Schmitt, John   31, 136
Schuh, Harry   82
Seahawks, Miami   111
Sebo, Steve   123
Sestak, Tom   75
Shamrocks, Boston   47
Shinnick, Don   24, 31
Shula, Don   24, 25, 35
Simpson, O. J.   76, (fig.) 77
Skogland, H. P.   49
Smith, Billy Ray   24, 31
Smith, Bubba   24, 25, 31, (fig.) 32
Smith, Dave   52, 97, 101
Smith, Charlie   18, 22, (fig.) 80
Snell, Matt   31, 32, 33, 34, 35, 131, 133, 136, (figs.) 19, 28, 29
Soda, Y. C. (Chet)   51
Speedie, Mac   92, 94, (fig.) 90
Spikes, Jack   52
Starr, Bart   35
Stirling, Scotty   82
Stofa, John   121
Storck, Carl   45
Stram, Hank (figs.) 62, 64
Sullivan, Billy   55-56
Sullivan, Dan   31
Super Bowl games:
    start of, 54
    1967, 65
    1968, 85
    1969, 26-36

Sutherland, Jock   44
Svihus, Bob   82

T

Talamini, Bob   31, 136
Taylor, Hugh (Bones)   102
Taylor, Lionel   87, 88
Taylor, Otis   69, (fig.) 66
Teresa, Tony   78
Texans, Dallas   52, 55, 61
Thomas, Danny   111
Thomas, Joe   112
Thorpe, Jim   42, 45
Tigers, Brooklyn   47
Tigers, Rochester   47
Titans, New York   91, 123, 128
Tolar, Charlie   101, 102
Torczon, LaVerne   70
Trenchard, Doggie   42
Tripucka, Frank   87, 88, 91
Trull, Don   102
Trumpy, John   121
Turner, Clyde (Bulldog), 127
Turner, Jim   19, 33, 133, (fig.) 129
Twilley, Howie   112

U

Unitas, John   23, 33, 35, (fig.) 29
Upshaw, Gene   85, (fig.) 81

V

Vogel, Bob   31
Volk, Rick   24, 31

W

Waddell, Rube   44
Walton, Sam   136
Warner, Glenn (Pop)   42
Warren, Jim   108, (fig.) 113
Webster, Dave   61
Webster, George   102, (fig.) 101
Wells, Warren   85
Werblin, David A. (Sonny) 37, 52-53, 128
Westmoreland, Dick   108
Wilson, George   111, (fig.) 112
Wilson, George, Jr.   112
Wilson, Ralph C.   70, 111, (fig.) 72
Wilson, Ralph, Jr.   49
Winter, Max   49
Wismer, Harry   49, 123, 127, (fig.) 126
Wood, Dick   112
Wood, Willie   69
Woodard, Milt   54

Y

Yankees, New York   47, 48
Young Men's Christian Association   42

Z

Zecker, Rich   82